The Little Book

of

Business Wisdom

The Little Book

of

Business Wisdom

*Rules of Success from More Than
50 Business Legends*

Edited by

Peter Krass

JOHN WILEY & SONS, INC.

NEW YORK · CHICHESTER · WEINHEIM · BRISBANE · SINGAPORE · TORONTO

ISBN 0-471-36979-9

Contents

Introduction

Imagine if past and present business legends such as Andrew Carnegie, Michael Dell, John D. Rockefeller, and Jack Welch were your personal drill sergeants, guiding you through your business paces. Imagine them marching before you, shouting short, pithy, and poignant commands to challenge you and to build you up. After all, a drill sergeant's purpose is not only to teach survival, but to conquer the enemy—however the enemy might manifest itself. Of course, I use the term *enemy* loosely. For us, it might be substituted for a megalomaniac boss, an unhappy customer, a daunting corporate ladder, a roller-coaster stock market, or even self-delusion, among endless other possibilities. But the real question is: What would the drill sergeant's commands be? Fortunately, many moguls and gurus have distilled their philosophies into hard-hitting lists of maxims—the ultimate commandments—and I have collected them here in *The Little Book of Business Wisdom.*

Sure, you could read a 750-page monster book on how to manage your career or your business, but perhaps those should be left to the academicians and their students with time to kill. The legends in this book deliver their formulas for success unencumbered by complicated jargon and fancy words—as

Lee Iacocca writes for his rule No. 3: "Say it in English and keep it short."

Some of the rules you'll discover are philosophical in nature, such as Iacocca's. Some are anecdotal: Michael Dell writes, "Swing for hits, not home runs: Business is like baseball. Go for the highest batting average rather than trying to hit a home run every time. If your competitor is batting .300, you want to bat .350 or .400." Or consider Peter Lynch's last rule on buying stocks: "Invest at least as much time and effort in choosing a new stock as you would in choosing a new refrigerator." Still other rules are very concrete: John D. Rockefeller writes, "Study diligently your capital requirements, and fortify yourself fully to cover possible setbacks, because you can absolutely count on meeting setbacks."

As you can imagine, these legendary business figures come from very different backgrounds and have very different priorities, which are reflected in their particular list. The differences—the topics and the attitudes are all over the place—are what make them both entertaining and instructive to read. *USA Today* founder Al Neuharth expounds on how to avoid burnout and stay fit, declaring, "Eat only when you're hungry; drink only when you're thirsty; sleep only when you're tired; screw only when you're horny." Holiday Inn's founder Kemmons Wilson opens his list with a slightly more prudent, but wry statement: "Work only a half a day; it makes no difference which half—it can be either the first 12 hours or the last 12 hours."

Certainly, some legends address the same topics, and if they happen to concur on a particular issue, we should take note because it is most likely essential to success. Take Andrew Carnegie and P. T. Barnum, one the king of steel, the other of entertainment. Carnegie writes, "And here is the prime condition for success, the great secret: concentrate your energy, thought, and capital exclusively upon the business in which you are engaged." Barnum also states unequivocally: "Don't scatter your powers." Others contradict each other. Advertising genius David Ogilvy admires well-organized people, writing, "The Duke of Wellington never went home until he had finished *all* the work on his desk." Newspaper magnate E. W. Scripps counters, "Never do anything today that you can put off till tomorrow." Hey, whatever works best.

Comparing and contrasting the business gurus with the executives in the trenches is another worthwhile exercise. You'll discover, for example, that Dale Carnegie, who penned the huge best-seller, *How to Win Friends and Influence People*, takes a far more subtle approach to criticizing others than does Dave Thomas, founder of Wendy's. Carnegie writes, "Call attention to people's mistakes indirectly," and "Let the other person save face." Whereas Thomas writes with a tougher tone, "Make 'em feel guilty when they do nothing," and "Don't put up with excuses." Although the authors have different viewpoints, an important point to recognize is that they have very definite opinions and maxims, which they *do not compromise*.

Returning to Iacocca, he concludes his list by stating, "When all is said and done, management is a code of values and judgments. And that's why, in the end, you have to be yourself." It is a fitting message to heed before you indulge: In the heat of the battle, don't try to follow every command these drill sergeants have barked out—take what's best for you without compromising your own beliefs.

PART I

Management Principles

Lee Iacocca

1924—

*B*orn and raised in a working-class neighborhood of Allen-
town, Pennsylvania, Lee Iacocca never left his tough up-
bringing behind—his street smarts aided his rise to the top of
Ford and Chrysler. He first stepped into the limelight in April of
1964 when he made the covers of both Time and Newsweek for
his introduction of the immensely popular Ford Mustang. His
celebrity status carried him to the presidency of the company in
1970, but then a fickle Henry Ford II, grandson of the legend,
fired him in 1978. Iacocca, who developed a rigid management
philosophy to survive good times and bad, was immediately
tapped to head a virtually bankrupt Chrysler. The company's
woes were ultimately turned around by the antithesis of the Mustang—the groundbreaking, hugely popular minivan.

My Little Commandments of Management

1. **Hire the Best.** Nothing will make a CEO look better than
   a talented management team. When I'm asked about how
   I turned Chrysler around, I always make the point that I
   didn't do it by myself—a lot of smart, dedicated people did
   it. Actually, since according to *Time* magazine my ego is as

big as all outdoors, I should probably take credit for having done all of it by myself.

2. **Get Your Priorities Straight and Keep a Hot List of What You're Trying to Do.** No matter how complex a business is, and ours is pretty complex, I believe you should be able to write down your top priorities on a single sheet of 8½-by-11 paper. It's always amazed me to see how many companies, even small ones, devote hours of effort and literally tons of paper to detailed plans of what they want the company to do over time. There are a lot of different names for them — Long Range Strategic Plans, Ten-Year Business Plans, Five-Year Profit Plans, and so forth. I guess if you've got a big staff and lots of extra time on your hands, it's not going to hurt you. But I've never seen a long-range business plan that couldn't be boiled down to a single page of priorities.

3. **Say It in English and Keep It Short.** Everyone has seen examples of bureaucratic double talk in written communication. You know what I mean — a long-winded document that takes the reader through two dozen options and alternatives and ends up with any one of six or seven different conclusions. Most of us associate this phenomenon with government bureaucracies. But take my word for it, a lot of double talk exists in corporations as well.

There are three factors behind the mumbo jumbo. First, the almost uncontrollable desire to tell all you know on any given subject. Second, the love of adjectives and adverbs over nouns and verbs. And third, the desire to impress your audience with your depth of vocabulary. I once read a fifteen-page paper that was tough to understand. I called in the author and asked him to explain what was in the tome he had written. He did it in two minutes flat. He identified what we were doing wrong, what we could do to fix it, and what he recommended. When he finished I asked him why he didn't write that in the paper the way he'd just said it to me. He didn't have an answer. All he said was: "I was taught that way." And he was an M.B.A. to boot.

Write the way you talk. If you don't talk that way, don't write that way.

4. **Never Forget the Line Makes the Money.** The political maneuvering between staff and line organiza-

> ### Savvy Leadership
>
> To help save an almost bankrupt Chrysler, Iacocca cut his salary to $1 as part of an austerity program. This also showed that he meant business when he told union officials, "Hey, boys, I've got a shotgun at your head. I've got thousands of jobs available at seventeen bucks an hour. I've got none at twenty."

tions is a wasteful and costly exercise. Every chief executive has got to come to grips with how he parcels out authority and accountability between these two groups. So I have a single axiom that helps me remember how to manage these often conflicting organizations. When the chips are down, it's the line organization that makes the money; the staff doesn't make a dime. I view the role of the staff as primarily to help the CEO do his job and to act as a catalyst to the line. If you really want to get a line group motivated, just float up a "staff idea" with the right amount of "Why didn't you guys think of that?"

5. **Lay Out the Size of the Playing Field.** I'm a strong believer in letting line operations "operate" — delegating to good people and then letting them do the job. But, you might ask, if the key managers are running the business, what's left for the CEO to do?

I think a big part of my job is what I call "defining the envelope," or setting the limits within which line management can operate on a relatively freewheeling basis. It's similar to a parent telling a child: "Play in the backyard but don't go past the gate and don't climb over the fence and don't invite anyone over." The child has the run of the yard, but the parent has prescribed limits on where he can go and what he can do.

As a CEO, I set limits. I set limits on the total amount of capital that can be spent—but not necessarily on how to spend it. I set limits on the number of executives I want on the payroll—but not who they are. I set limits on the amount of R & D spending I'm willing to support—but not the projects that are funded. And I establish the company priorities, which represent the limits or parameters that set the direction of the whole line effort.

6. **Keep Some Mavericks Around.** All CEOs should worry about getting fed a single point of view: that is, a party line that has been filtered, refiltered, homogenized, pasteurized, and synthesized—what we call "cooking the pudding." Without differences in viewpoint, and openness to constructive expression of these differences, a corporation can be led into a lot of bad decisions. There is a real risk in telling the CEO only what he wants to hear and never having any disagreements in his presence.

To guard against this risk, I've always tried to keep some smart people around me who are contrarians, who for whatever reason will not accept very much at face value and are not impressed by the rationale that something is being done in a certain way because it's always been done that way.

7. **Stay in Business During Alterations.** A lot of CEO surveys indicate that long-range planning and strategic planning are seen as among the most important responsibilities for a CEO. I'm not going to argue with that, but I've always felt that making sure you're maximizing earnings today is also a key responsibility. It's easy, I think, for an organization to get mesmerized by long-range plans. On paper, at least, they're neat and squared-off—and always work.

8. **Remember the Fundamentals.** I have always been a fan of Vince Lombardi, the late great leader of the Green Bay Packers. Although his teams had a fairly versatile offensive game, at least for that period of time, their real strength lay in their adherence to the fundamentals of playing solid football: blocking and tackling, good play execution, and mental discipline. They weren't the fanciest football team of their day, but to watch them run a power sweep with the linemen pulling out and blocking was to see a thing of beauty. It was also a devastatingly effective offensive weapon.

When all is said and done, management is a code of values and judgments. And that's why, in the end, you have to be yourself.

Which brings me to the best rule of management: Pick a style that you're comfortable with and stick with it. You can have role models, but don't try to be somebody else. Be yourself, stay natural and dammit, smile once in a while!

Bill Gates
1955–

Today's richest man in the world and software mogul was in eighth grade when he encountered his first computer; he's also a college dropout. After two years at Harvard, where he enjoyed playing poker over going to classes, Bill Gates dropped out in 1975 to start Microsoft with his high school buddy, Paul Allen. Their first project was writing software for a home-brew computer, and their first big coup was winning the contract in 1980 to develop an operating system for IBM's personal computer. They then expanded rapidly into word processing and spreadsheet software, going public in 1986. After a bout with cancer, Allen left the company and today Gates is chairman. Although the company lost an antitrust case brought against them, Gates remains an aggressive visionary who devoutly believes in the power of digital tools.

New Rules for the Age of Information

To make digital information flow an intrinsic part of your company, here are twelve key steps:

For *knowledge work:*

1. Insist that communication flow through the organization over e-mail so that you can act on news with reflexlike speed.

2. Study sales data online to find patterns and share insights easily. Understand overall trends and personalize service for individual customers.
3. Use PCs for business analysis, and shift knowledge workers into high-level thinking work about products, services, and profitability.
4. Use digital tools to create cross-departmental virtual teams that can share knowledge and build on each other's ideas in real time, worldwide. Use digital systems to capture corporate history for use by anyone.
5. Convert every paper process to a digital process, eliminating administrative bottlenecks and freeing knowledge workers for more important tasks.

For *business operations:*

> ### Savvy Leadership
> Twice a year, Gates would personally visit archrival WordPerfect's best customers, seeking to understand why they chose WordPerfect over Microsoft's Word.

6. Use digital tools to eliminate single-task jobs or change them into value-added jobs that use the skills of a knowledge worker.
7. Create a digital feedback loop to improve the efficiency of physical processes and improve the quality of the products and services created. Every employee should be able to easily track all the key metrics.
8. Use digital systems to route customer complaints immediately to the people who can improve a product or service.
9. Use digital communications to redefine the nature of your business and the boundaries around your business. Become larger and more substantial or smaller and more intimate as the customer situation warrants.

For *commerce:*

10. Trade information for time. Decrease cycle time by using digital transactions with all suppliers and partners, and transform every business process into just-in-time delivery.

11. Use digital delivery of sales and service to eliminate the middleman from customer transactions. If you're a middleman, use digital tools to add value to transactions.

12. Use digital tools to help customers solve problems for themselves, and reserve personal contact to respond to complex, high-value customer needs.

Smart Habits

While en route to an unfamiliar place, Gates voraciously reads books and magazine articles about it—the material is often recommended by local managers—and then asks plenty of follow-up questions once he is there. While in India, he discovered that there were 14 distinct languages and realized Microsoft's products had to be much more localized, ultimately fueling sales.

Managing Unhappy Customers

I recommend the following approach to integrating customer complaints and wish lists into product and service development:

1. Focus on your most unhappy customers.
2. Use technology to gather rich information on their unhappy experiences with your product and to find out what they want you to put into the product.

3. Use technology to drive the news to the right people in
   a hurry.

If you do these three things, you'll turn those draining,
bad news experiences into an exhilarating process of improving your product or service. Unhappy customers are always a
concern. They're also your greatest opportunity.

Michael S. Dell

1965–

*M*ichael Dell's direct business model, which involves selling customized products directly to the consumer and keeping inventory to a minimum, has revolutionized the way in which companies do business as they attempt to emulate Dell's success. Dell Computer's stock was up more than 3,000 percent in the 1990s—not bad for a college dropout. His mother was a stockbroker and his father an orthodontist, who wanted their son to become a doctor. Although he enrolled at the University of Texas as a premed student, computers were Dell's first love, and in his first semester in 1983 he started buying old computers and upgrading them for resale. That next summer he sold $180,000 worth and never returned to school. Dell took the company public in 1988 and maintains a competitive edge by infusing his company with a sense of urgency.

The Competitive Edge

- Think about the customer, not the competition: Competitors represent your industry's past, as, over the years, collective habits become ingrained. Customers are your future, representing new opportunities, ideas, and avenues for growth.

- Work to maintain a healthy sense of urgency and crisis: This doesn't mean that you want to fabricate deadlines or keep people so stressed that they quickly burn out. Set the bar slightly higher than you normally would, so that your people can achieve aggressive goals by working smarter.
- Turn your competition's greatest strength into a weakness: Much as every great athlete has an Achilles' heel, so, too, do all great companies. Study the competition's "game": Exploit its weakness by exposing its greatest strength.
- Be opportunistic, but also be fast: Look to find opportunity, especially when it isn't readily apparent. Focusing on the customer doesn't mean that you should ignore the competition. If something that your competition did or didn't do provided you with an opportunity today, would you recognize it and be able to act on it immediately? Today a competitive win can be decided literally one day at a time. You have to act fast, be ready, then be ready to change—fast.

> ### Savvy Leadership
> To make sure that all employees became Internet-literate, Dell had posters hung in all high-traffic areas of their buildings. On the poster was Michael Dell, posing as Uncle Sam, with the caption, "Michael wants YOU to know the Net!"

- Swing for hits, not home runs: Business is like baseball. Go for the highest batting average rather than trying to hit a home run every time. If your competitor is batting .300, you want to bat .350 or .400. No one's batting 1.000, so you can't worry about it. What you want to focus on is being the best as often as you can. Because there's no such thing as a grand slam product or technology that lasts forever, your competitive edge must come from strategic execution, and from gaining knowledge, studying the economics of your business, and ensuring the flow of information throughout your organization.

- Be the hunter, not the hunted: Success is a dangerous thing, as we are at once invincible and vulnerable. Always strive to keep your team focused on growing the business and on winning and acquiring new business. Even though your company may be leading the market, you never want your people to act as though you are. That leads to complacency, and complacency kills. Encourage people to think, "This is good. This worked. Now how can we take what we've proven and use it to win new business?" There's a big difference between asking that and asking, "How can we defend our existing accounts?"

Charles B. Wang

1944–

*C*harles Wang, born in China, is cofounder, chairman, and CEO of the world's third largest independent software maker, Computer Associates International (CA). After the Chinese Communist revolution in 1949, Wang and his family fled to the United States. They found themselves in a Queens, New York, housing project. Wang attended Queens College, where he earned degrees in both mathematics and physics. When the time came to choose a profession, Wang settled on becoming a computer programmer; he concluded that because there were so many help-wanted ads for them, this was a growing industry. When the company for which he was working decided to sell its software division in 1975, he and friend Russell Artzt went for it. Wang, who strives to be in sync with technology and wants his company to match up with the best, took CA public in 1981 and has used the proceeds to gobble up some 60 other companies.

Sync or Swim: Seven Steps to Being the Best

1. **Benchmark to determine the world standard.** Some organization has to be the best, why not yours? Find the world champion in every process—technical and otherwise—that

you measure. Do the benchmarks to determine how your performance compares. Recalibrate your goals accordingly.

Outrageous Promotion

Early on in building his business, Wang would pick 20 pages from the Yellow Pages, drink three cups of coffee, and cold-call every potential customer before going to the bathroom.

Savvy Leadership

Wang banned the use of e-mail from 10:00 A.M. until noon and from 2:00 P.M. until 4:00 P.M. to force face-to-face interaction among his people.

---

2. **Map your processes.** Break activities down into processes. Identify the inefficiencies. Reinvent. For each step, ask whether customers, if given a choice, would pay for it.

3. **Get your people focused on external reality.** The issues are customers and competitors. Define a clear vision that creates a sense of urgency. Insist that people accept responsibility for their own behavior.

4. **Start with the hardest part.** Distinguish what needs to be done from how hard it is to do it. The most difficult steps are generally the most important. Model the attitude that if something really needs to be done, the difficulty of doing it is irrelevant.

5. **Set the goals high and then double them.** Your people will rise to the challenge if you support them properly. Set the goal but don't tell them how to do it. Their ideas will be better than yours. If people fail to reach the goal, don't punish them, adjust your support.

6. **Let go and watch.** You can't do it alone so kick back and enjoy.

7. **Wave laurels; don't rest on them.** When you're on top of the mountain, it's natural to want to relax. Take a minute and enjoy the view. But hang on. It's windy up there. You won't have privacy for long. Your competitors—benchmarks in hand—are within hailing distance.

John Erik Jonsson

1901–1995

*J*ohn Jonsson, the son of Swedish immigrants, cofounded the *electronics giant Texas Instruments (TI) and served as mayor of Dallas from 1964 to 1971. Originally, he was from New Jersey, where his father owned a cigar and candy shop. While studying engineering at Rensselaer Polytechnic Institute, he repaired radios at night to make money. Jonsson went to work for the Aluminum Company of America in 1922 and then was recruited in 1930 to manage a laboratory of Geophysical Service, Inc., which was based in Dallas and developed seismographic instruments for finding oil and gas. Eventually, Jonsson and a partner bought the company, and in 1951, the company's name was changed to TI. A master strategist, he believed in* programming *every function in the company, based on proven management principles.*

Management Principles

1. We write down and try to see that as many people in our organization as possible understand the basic objectives of TI. We re-examine and restate these objectives regularly to meet changing needs and changing times.

2. To achieve sound growth, we believe that we must have a well-conceived and well-executed planning program aimed toward the achievement of TI objectives. Our basic objectives are long-range. When planning begins, it may be necessary to think only of the short-range, but as soon afterward as possible, we must lengthen the range and broaden the scope of all our plans.

3. We must organize to implement our plans fully. The scope of the organizing job should be comprehensive enough to include adequate handling and dovetailing of all functions requisite to execution of the plans. Such functions as research and development, its staffing, and its laboratories should be carefully organized and programmed. Similarly, our financial programming must be early and comprehensive enough to permit proper sequential staging of individual steps, since the sequence may be as important as the individual steps themselves.

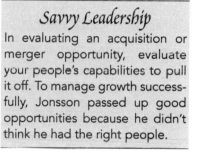

Savvy Leadership

In evaluating an acquisition or merger opportunity, evaluate your people's capabilities to pull it off. To manage growth successfully, Jonsson passed up good opportunities because he didn't think he had the right people.

4. As part of the planning program, our management personnel requirements through all levels should be considered far ahead of actual needs, so that the balanced procurement of required individuals can sometimes be achieved as much as several years in advance.

5. Keep flexible, keep current. Change our plans whenever circumstances require. Plans are not axiomatic of themselves, and a planning program whose original premises are wrong

or obsolete may be worse than none. Re-examine regularly the what, when, where, why, and how of all plans.

6. Since our growth pattern includes diversified product lines or services for a variety of markets, decentralized product divisions are the best organizational answer for us.

7. Each new product division we create must be as completely and capably staffed as the parent from which it sprang. All product divisions should be as complete in function and as autonomous as possible and should operate within the over-all limits established by central management.

8. Our central management staff must be strong and, in addition to performing general management duties and the usual specialization and service assistance to product divisions, should have the prime responsibility for formalizing the policies and procedures within whose framework the entire organization must function. This staff should take as one of its special responsibilities our purely long-term and over-all planning.

9. It is our purpose not to waste energy in research and development, or in manufacturing or marketing a product line to which we are unwilling to devote the time and money necessary for success. Especially in product lines obtained by mergers and acquisitions, accomplishment of the desired objectives will be harder, slower, and often more expensive than with those developed internally.

10. Timing is of the essence in everything we undertake. A research and development program or an entry into new markets that comes too early or late can defeat the original intent. The vital importance of timing can be seen directly in financing, for example, since it is reflected immediately in terms and rates.

11. Our performance as a company will be limited only by the quality of our people.

I should like to amplify this last point, since it is the most important of all. We have discussed products and services and delineated some management principles we believe to be sound. However, little has been said about the men and women on whose efforts our hopes of future success are based. We have tried to surround ourselves with people of quality and ability who can be integrated into a powerful team moving toward common, clearly defined and understood goals. Because we have faith and confidence in the capabilities of our people, we have set our targets high. And these difficult challenges have always sparked their creativeness and will to succeed. While we have attempted to make rewards as directly proportional to accomplishment as possible, the personnel of Texas Instruments have shown a loyalty and willingness to produce beyond reasonable expectations. This, together with the understanding support of customers and stockholders, has provided those of us in TI's top management with a challenge of our own. We must try to grow with our company, to develop a statesmanship in business management worthy of the confidence and respect of all.

Harold S. Geneen

1910–1997

$\mathcal{H}$arold Geneen is regarded as one of the most brilliant businesspeople to lead a multinational conglomerate. Born in Britain, he and his family moved to the United States when he was less than a year old. After a stint as a page on Wall Street, he pursued an accounting career and went through a number of finance jobs (and companies). Geneen was hired as an executive vice president of Raytheon in 1956 and was given the mission to turn the ailing company around, which he did. When he was recruited for ITT's presidency in 1959, he inherited a stodgy telecommunications company. Geneen, however, transformed it into a powerhouse that included 150 affiliated companies operating in 57 countries. Although he was managing a complex organization, his precepts were as simple as: Avoid pretensions and ego trips.

Succeeding in a Business Career

Some time ago, speaking at the Wharton School of Business Administration, I was asked how one should go about succeeding in a business career. I told the students that one should move around and gain experience in his or her early years and then settle down to a chosen career at age thirty or thirty-five. That would give a person a career of some thirty or thirty-five years. In that time, the top management of a company is likely to turn over three or four times. So there would always be room for a good manager. All a young person had to do was to pick his or her job and start working toward it. As I said about *all* management, including the management of one's life: Decide what it is you want to do, and start doing it.

If I were to amend that answer today and try to sum up what I have come to believe over a long career in business, I would put forth these personal precepts on how to manage:

- You must play by the rules, going through the channels of the company structure, taking no shortcuts; but you don't have to *think* by the rules. It would be a great mistake to confine your imagination to the way things have always been done. In fact, it would consign you to the mediocrity of the marketplace.
- Avoid all pretensions. Doing things for "show" will backfire on you and turn the whole flavor of your enterprise rancid. Avoid ego trips, office politics, and acting a part that is not really you.
- Remember: Facts from paper are not the same as facts from people. The reliability of the person giving you the facts is as important as the facts themselves. Keep in mind that facts are seldom facts, but what people think are facts, heavily tinged with assumptions.
- You must find out everything essential by yourself. As a manager, you are entitled to a straight answer to a straight question, and you will usually get it when your question is right. The right question comes from many sources and must be assembled in your own head, perhaps for the first time.
- The good guys in your organization want you to ask the right question, because they can and want to answer it. Then you can all move forward together.

- Only the phonies will squirm when confronted by questions that go straight to the heart of the matter, and it is your job as a manager to recognize the phonies and to get rid of them. The good guys will expect it of you.
- No one is going to tell you the answer or solution to any problem in advance of your questioning. It is the nature of organization and the interaction of the hierarchy that usually stop a bright man from breaking the code of getting along with his peers.

Smart Habits

Whether you are a CEO or low-level manager, Geneen warns that you must screen your actions for personal prejudice and vanity; for example, if you start worrying about the view from your office or whom you sit next to in a meeting, it's time to evaluate your ego.

- When you are the man or woman in charge, you and only you must make the decisions, particularly the close ones. That's what you are being paid for, whether you head a task force, a department, or a whole company. Your decisions should be based upon the facts of the situation. The facts are the authority. Because you are in charge, *you* are entitled to be right or wrong, but it must be you. Your commands will be honored and respected, but they must be *your* commands. You are not entitled to announce decisions or give commands by proxy, by allowing someone else to speak for you.

PART II

~

Leadership Secrets

T. Boone Pickens

1928–

T. Boone Pickens built the largest independently owned oil
and gas company in the United States, Mesa Petroleum;
and yet Pickens recalls that in the fourth grade he was so shy,
the girl next to him had to read his homework out loud when he
was chosen by the teacher. After studying geology at Oklahoma
State, he took a job with Phillips Petroleum in 1951 as an oil
well–site geologist. It was not long before he became disillu-
sioned with the company's bureaucracy and quit at the age of
26, even though he had a wife, two young children, and a third
on the way. Pickens lived out of his station wagon as he drove
around Texas prospecting choice land to drill and raising the
financing to do it. In 1956, with two partners and $2,500, Pick-
ens founded Mesa Petroleum and became a maverick leader,
who thrived on risk and took on the big oil companies.

The Art of Leadership

- Master the art of leadership. A wise woman, retired U.S.
Navy Admiral Grace Hopper, expressed my philosophy suc-
cinctly when she said, "You don't manage people. You manage things. You *lead* people." She was right. The important
part of being a leader is what goes on inside your own

mind—what you do to yourself, not what you do to others. Part of leadership is taking risks and building confidence in yourself. You have to serve many apprenticeships throughout your life. Show me somebody who won't serve an apprenticeship, and I'll show you somebody who won't go very far. At Mesa, people who are good, strong players find their apprenticeships to be surprisingly short.

- Concentrate on the goals, not the size of the organization. You can't measure a place by size unless it's a football stadium. At Mesa, we work short-handed. That way people have a greater opportunity to advance and less time for office politics.
- Forget about age, which means giving the young people a chance. I have a bias toward youth, but I also think that youth is a state of mind. You can be old at 30 or young at 70. I am interested in whether a person can do the job. Mesa personnel know this well, and it is a great boost for morale. The average age of all Mesa employees is 36.
- Keep things informal. Talking is the natural way to do business. Writing is great for keeping records and pinning down details, but talk generates ideas. Great things come from our luncheon meetings, which consist of a sandwich, a cup of soup, and a good idea or two. No martinis.
- Keep communication lines open. Communication is crucial—not the formal stuff, but frequent conversation among the people who make the decisions. My people know that they can talk to me, no matter how busy I am. So when it's time to make a decision I'm ready, with no need for lengthy presentations. Communication means no surprises. I hate surprises.
- Play by the rules. This applies not only outside the company, but inside too. I'm disturbed by what I've seen in the last sev-

eral years, with people being asked to take early retirement in their 50s while the C.E.O. stays on past the mandatory retirement age of 65. Are any of us so valuable that we should be exempt from the rules?

- Hire the best. I choose people for their intelligence, attitude, and enthusiasm — people who can do a job better than I can. I never load myself so that people under me aren't challenged. But if you aren't a worker, you won't make it with me. The same goes for people who are not comfortable in a fast-moving operation, who want more time to think or maybe procrastinate. My advice to our people is: If you aren't happy, leave. As for people who drink on the job, steal, or carry on an interoffice relationship, I'll fire them on the spot.

> ### Smart Habits
> Never set psychological limits for yourself, Pickens advises; for example, don't set a particular job level, salary amount, or net worth as a satisfactory career goal. Although you may change your mind later, that original goal, while only in your mind, can become as great a barrier as a real roadblock.

- Keep fit. Physical fitness is an essential part of the best-run companies — and that includes C.E.O.s. I never had a weight problem because I did things in moderation. But I gradually got out of shape, which is easy to do in your late 30s or early 40s. In 1972 I began to work out. I jogged and took up racquetball seriously. All those things you hear about being in shape are true: I felt better. My stamina improved and so did my powers of concentration. I was getting a lot more done each day and still had energy to burn.

Keeping fit has economic as well as spiritual and psychological benefits. In 1979 Mesa built a first-class athletic facility equipped as well as any commercial health center. About three-quarters of Mesa's employees, me included, participate in the fitness program. The Fitness Center saves Mesa more than $200,000 in insurance claims annually. Our records show that employees who exercise regularly average $173 in medical bills a year, whereas it costs $434 for inactive employees. Exercisers average 27 hours of sick leave per year; non-exercisers, 44 hours.

- Finally, enjoy it. We may work hard, but there are no stomachaches. We laugh a lot. If we screw up, then we all screwed up. We move quickly, which often creates an advantage. Some companies operate on a two-, five-, or ten-year plan. At Mesa, we're a different company every two years.

John F. Welch, Jr.

1935–

*B*ack in 1973, Jack Welch boldly stated on his employee evaluation that his long-range goal was to be CEO. Welch, whose father was a train conductor, grew up in blue-collar Salem, Massachusetts. After studying at the University of Massachusetts and at the University of Illinois, where he earned a Ph.D. in chemical engineering, he joined General Electric (GE) as a junior engineer. However, he quit just over a year later in 1961, because he couldn't stand the bureaucracy. Fortunately, his boss convinced him to stay. Twenty years later he did, indeed, take over as CEO of GE. Welch, who has a definitive philosophy for corporate revolution, was quickly dubbed "Neutron Jack" by Newsweek magazine as he reengineered the company, either eliminating or divesting one-third of the company's workforce (170,000 jobs) over the next five years.

Leading a Revolution

- You've got to be prepared for massive resistance. Incremental change doesn't work well in the type of transformation GE has gone through. If your change isn't big enough, revolutionary enough, the bureaucracy can beat you.
- You've got to be hard to be soft. You have to demonstrate the ability to make the hard, tough decisions—closing plants,

divesting, delayering—if you want to have any credibility when you try to promote soft values.

- Every organization needs values, but a lean organization needs them even more. When you strip away the support systems of staffs and layers, people have to change their habits and expectations, or else the stress will just overwhelm them.

> ### Savvy Leadership
> To inspire and motivate the troops, Welch spontaneously sends a handwritten note to those in need of encouragement, whether they be direct reports or hourly workers. He faxes the note directly to them and then puts the original in the mail.

- You've got to be out in front of crowds, repeating yourself over and over again, never changing your message no matter how much it bores you.
- You need an overarching message, something big but simple and understandable. Whatever it is—*we're going to be No. 1 or No. 2,* or *fix/close/sell, or boundaryless*—every idea you present must be something you could get across easily at a cocktail party with strangers.
- The three most important things you need to measure in a business are customer satisfaction, employee satisfaction, and cash flow.

GE Values Guide on Wallet-Size Card

GE employees are required to carry the GE Values Guide on a wallet-size card.

GE Leaders . . . Always with Unyielding Integrity:

- Have a Passion for Excellence and Hate Bureaucracy
- Are Open to Ideas from Anywhere . . . and Committed to Work-Out
- Live Quality . . . and Drive Cost and Speed for Competitive Advantage
- Have the Self-Confidence to Involve Everyone and Behave in a Boundaryless Fashion
- Create a Clear, Simple, Reality-Based Vision . . . and Communicate It to All Constituencies
- Have Enormous Energy and the Ability to Energize Others
- Stretch . . . Set Aggressive Goals . . . Reward Progress . . . Yet Understand Accountability and Commitment
- See Change as Opportunity . . . Not Threat
- Have Global Brains . . . and Build Diverse and Global Teams

Robert Townsend

1920–

*R*obert Townsend, author of the best-selling Up the Orga-nization, has always promoted employee independence. *The Townsend family was imbued with a rebellious spirit; an American ancestor was a revolutionary spy who worked against the British. After earning an English literature degree at Princeton University, Townsend also served in the military during World War II. In 1948, he joined Hertz American Express International and became senior vice president of the investment and international banking operations for American Express. While there, he observed how the cash-rich company could afford to make mistakes; he later incorporated many of those no-no's into his leadership philosophy. In 1962, he left to become president and chairman of Avis, Inc.*

No-No's

Reserved parking spaces. If you're so bloody important, you better be first one in the office. Besides, you'll meet a nice class of people in the employees' parking lot.

Special-quality stationery for the boss and his elite.

Muzak, except in the areas where the work is only suitable for mental defectives.

Bells and buzzers (even telephones can be made to signal with lights).

Company shrinks. Unless it's really optional, and the shrink reports only to the patient, and suitable precautions have been taken to make sure the personnel department can't tap into the data.

Outside directorships and trusteeships for the chief executive. Give up all those non-jobs. You can't even run your own company, dummy.

Company plane. It's just a variation of the company-paid golf club, and the big office with three secretaries. Another line drawn through the company between the Brahmins and the untouchables. And the plane's always in Palm Beach, Augusta, Aspen, or Las Vegas when the business needs it. Best thing about it: if it has only one pilot, someday he'll get ptomaine with a whole load of "top" management aboard . . .

Manager's Monthly. Or any other time-consuming report imposed on the troops by "top" management. It's a joke because it consumes ten pounds of energy to produce each ounce of misunderstanding.

Except in poker, bridge, and similar play-period activities, **don't con anybody.**

Not your wife
Not your children
Not your employees
Not your customers
Not your stockholders
Not your boss
Not your associates

Not your suppliers
Not your regulatory authorities
Not even your competitors

Don't con yourself either.
Social relations within the firm. Okay with your peers. But
not with people who report to you. You'll inevitably see
more of the ones you like—and they may not be the best
performers. Your own performance depends on your ability to be just. Don't make it any tougher than it is.

Hiring. To keep an organization
young and fit, don't hire anyone until everybody's so over-
worked they'll be glad to
see the newcomer no matter
where he sits.

Savvy Leadership
To blur the us-them line between
headquarters and the front lines,
Townsend forced all HQ managers to go to car rental school,
and then to wear Avis's red rental
uniforms to honor the frontline
counter workers.

Trade associations—as a chance
to fix prices, and allocate
customers and markets with
your friendly competitors.
Antitrust laws are different: you're not innocent until
proven guilty. If all your customers are north of Main Street
and all your competitor's customers are south of Main
Street, you're both guilty by inference. And nobody has to
prove the two of you ever communicated in any way. Treble
damages. Jail. So watch it, bubele.

Conventions. The public relations dream: much money,
time, and energy signifying nothing. The best way is to
ignore them. The next best way is to send one line man
(rotate the assignment like kitchen police). On his
return, ask him to make a thirty-second all-inclusive oral

report to the weekly staff meeting covering everything of significance that he heard, saw, and learned. The worst way is to give your P.R. department a blank check and tell them to make a big splash.

House organs. Spend the money making stockholders out of your employees and then sending them (along with the other stockholders) honest reports on how the company's really doing: good and bad. Reading a house organ is like going down in warm maple syrup for the third time.

> ### Smart Habits
>
> Townsend, who preached against the delegation of grunt work, did not have a personal secretary and answered his own phone.

Greed. To increase our share of the market a few years ago, I was on the verge of approving the start-up of a new subsidiary—which would compete with our bread-and-butter business—at discount prices. To verify my own brilliance I tried the idea out on a tall, rangy regional vice-president named Stepnowski. After hearing the plan described in some detail, he sank the whole project with one sentence: "I don't know what *you* call it, but we Polacks call that 'pissing in the soup.'"

Office Party, How Not to Do the Annual

1. *Start it at 5 p.m. instead of noon, so the company doesn't lose any man-hours.*
2. *Invite spouses so bosses and their secretaries don't enjoy dancing together.*

(Continued)

3. *Make sure the top brass either doesn't show or puts in a token appearance—underscoring the difference between them and the rest of us playful, indolent darkies.*

4. *Invite clients and suppliers to help reinforce their contempt for your company.*

5. *Skimp on the setting. A third-rate roadhouse is always good.*

6. *Cut corners on the food and booze. Two-day-old hors d'oeuvres left over from a wedding, a tray of Manhattans, and a mystery punch ought to do it.*

7. *Save money on the music. Better than a phonograph is a tin-eared accordionist whose idea of a new number is "I Could Have Danced All Night."*

8. *Kill two birds by combining it with the annual quarter-century-club party. Then all your employees can see living examples (you should excuse the expression) of what twenty-five years in your outfit will do to what were once healthy human beings.*

9. *Better yet, turn the whole thing over to the head of the personnel department and tell him to use his best judgment.*

John H. Patterson

1844–1922

*C*onsidered the father of modern salesmanship, John Patterson was a great communicator and motivator who founded
the National Cash Register Company (NCR). After attending
Dartmouth College, he eventually went to work managing a
coal yard and a company store for the employees. The store was
always in the red because the cashiers were skimming, and it
was then that Patterson decided to give a new contraption a
try—Ritty's Incorruptible Cashier, which tabulated sales. He
bought two registers in 1882, and in 1884 he decided to buy the
entire company, changing the name to NCR. His sales inno-
vations included establishing an equitable sales quota system,
codifying sales talk, and producing one of the first sales manu-
als that surely included his principles for communicating.

Principles for Idea-Conveying

If I should reduce my principles of idea-conveying to a creed,
it would run something in this fashion:

1. The nerves from the eyes to the brain are many times
   larger than those from the ears to the brain. Therefore,

when possible to *use a picture* instead of words, use one and make the words mere connectives for the pictures.

2. Confine the attention to the exact subject by drawing outlines and putting in the divisions; then we make certain that we are all talking about the same thing.

Extreme Measures

Patterson was known to throw away everything in his executives' desks, including personal items, to make them start afresh.

---

3. Aim for dramatic effects either in speaking or writing—study them out beforehand. This holds the attention.

4. Red is the best color to attract and hold attention, therefore use plenty of it.

5. Few words—short sentences—small words—big ideas.

6. Tell why as well as how.

7. Do not be afraid of big type and do not put too much on a page.

8. Do not crowd ideas in speaking or writing. No advertisement is big enough for two ideas.

9. Before you try to convince anyone else, make sure that you are convinced, and if you cannot convince yourself, drop the subject. Do not try to "put over anything."

10. Tell the truth.

John D. Rockefeller

1839–1937

*R*ockefeller's father was to have said, *"I cheat my boys every chance I get. I want to make 'em sharp."* Clearly, Rockefeller had a sharp eye for deal making; fortunately, though, he later turned to philanthropy and gave away more than $500 million. In 1859, Rockefeller and a partner opened a commission house in Cleveland, the same year that oil was discovered in western Pennsylvania. Crude oil and related products were soon bought and sold by Rockefeller, and he quickly grasped the importance of oil refining. With his brother, William, and two other partners, he founded the Standard Oil Company in 1870. By the 1880s, Rockefeller, who relied on patience, courage, and good old common sense, controlled over 90 percent of the U.S. oil refinery business (and was eventually declared in violation of The Sherman Anti-Trust Act).

The American Businessman

- The man who starts out simply with the idea of getting rich won't succeed; you must have a larger ambition.
- Sometimes I feel that we Americans think we can find a short road to success, and it may appear that often this feat is accomplished; but the real efficiency in work comes from knowing your facts and building upon that sure foundation.

- It takes infinite patience and courage to compel men to have confidence in you. I believe I have both of these qualities, and I also believe that they are the secrets of my success.
- There is no mystery in business success. The great industrial leaders have told again and again the plain and obvious fact that there can be no permanent success without fair dealing that leads to widespread confidence in the man himself, and that is the real capital we all prize and work for.
- It is not always the easiest of tasks to induce strong, forceful men to agree. It has always been our policy to hear patiently and discuss frankly until the last shred of evidence is on the table, before trying to reach a conclusion and to decide finally upon a course of action.
- Look ahead. It is surprising how many bright business men go into important undertakings with little or no study of the controlling conditions they risk their all upon.
- As I began my business life as a bookkeeper, I learned to have great respect for figures and facts, no matter how small they were.
- It is to be remembered that ofttimes, the most difficult competition comes, not from the strong, the intelligent, the conservative competitor, but from the man who is holding on by the eyelids and is ignorant of his costs, and anyway, he's got to "keep running or bust."

Smart Habits

After a spirited conversation, whether with ally or enemy, Rockefeller would repeat to himself over and over the important points made by others. He disciplined himself to be a great listener to retain important information for later use. Each night he would also talk out loud to his pillow, reviewing the day's events and voicing his concerns.

- Study diligently your capital requirements, and fortify yourself fully to cover possible set-backs, because you can absolutely count on meeting set-backs. Be sure that you are not deceiving yourself at any time about actual conditions.
- Good old-fashioned common sense has always been a mighty rare commodity.

J. C. Penney
1875–1971

J. C. Penney's first business venture as a butcher failed because he refused to supply meat to hotels that sold liquor. In 1902 he started working for a dry goods store in Kemmerer, Wyoming, and was eventually allowed to buy into one-third of the business. Eight years later, he had opened 13 stores of his own, calling them the Golden Rule Stores. The name of the stores was changed to JCPenney in 1913, and Penney, whose winning formula was built on hard work and honesty, was operating 175 stores in 1917. The rapid growth was achieved by requiring the store managers to own 33 percent of their store, an early form of franchising, along with Penney's most ingenious revolution of creating a central warehouse and corresponding inventory control system to increase buying power and reduce costs.

Six Principles for Winning

Preparation Wins. A man must know all about his business. He must know a little more than any other man knows. As a rule we achieve what we prepare for.

Hard Work Wins. The only kind of luck that any man is justified in banking on is hard work, which is made up of sacrifice, persistent effort, and dogged determination. Growth is never by mere chance. The success we build will be the achievement of our united efforts.

Honesty Wins. This must be not only the kind of honesty that keeps a man's fingers out of his neighbor's till, but the finer honesty that will not allow a man to give less than his best, the kind of honesty that makes him count not his hours but his duties and opportunities, and constantly urges him to increase his efficiency.

Confidence in Men Wins. I have found my most successful associates by giving men responsibility, by making them feel that I relied upon them; and those who have

> ### Savvy Leadership
>
> When interviewing prospective hires, Penney made the job sound as unattractive as possible to see if they flinched, to determine who was timid and who was not. On the other hand, if an interviewee jumped at the chance too eagerly, they were also scratched from the list.

proved to be unworthy have only caused the others, who far outnumbered them, to stand in a clearer light. This principle, at least in a measure, is responsible for the success of our mercantile organization. Use good business judgment, of course. Do not throw away common sense, but believe in yourself, and trust your fellows.

The Spirit Wins. One of the wisest men who ever lived said, "The letter killeth, the spirit giveth life." Every enterprise I have been interested in demonstrates this fact. It is the spirit of the individuals comprising any organization, the spirit of the pioneers in any enterprise or endeavor—that spirit of men and women who are at the foundation of such organizations and enterprises—which will solve problems, conquer difficulties, and achieve individual and collective successes.

Extreme Measures

Penney, whose stores were called the Golden Rule Stores before being renamed after himself, did not permit his employees to drink or to smoke.

A *Practical Application of the Golden Rule Wins.* As enunciated by the Master Teacher on the hillsides of Judea nearly two thousand years ago, the golden rule runs, "Therefore all things whatsoever ye would that men should do to you, do ye even so to them; for this is the law and the prophets."

PART III

~

Qualities for Personal Advancement

David Ogilvy

1911–

*B*orn and raised in Scotland, advertising genius David Ogilvy recalled, "When I was six, he [his father] required that I should drink a glass of raw blood every day." Early in his career, Ogilvy bounced through several jobs, including that of a chef and a stove salesman. Eventually, he went to work doing research for a London advertising agency, and then he emigrated to America in search of adventure. Ogilvy found work with Dr. George Gallup, creator of the Gallup Poll. When World War II broke out, he used his position with Gallup to gather information and to advise the British Government on American opinions. It was not until after a stint as a farmer in Amish country that, in 1952, Ogilvy finally founded Ogilvy & Mather. In the wild world of advertising, Ogilvy discovered that finding the right people was essential to his success.

Qualities I Admire

1. I admire people who work hard, who bite the bullet. I dislike passengers who don't pull their weight in the boat. It is more fun to be overworked than to be underworked. There is an economic factor built into hard work. The harder you work, the fewer employees we need, and the

more profit we make. The more profit we make, the more money becomes available for all of us.

2. I admire people with first-class brains, because you cannot run a great advertising agency without brainy people. But brains are not enough unless they are combined with *intellectual honesty*.

3. I have an inviolable rule against employing nepots and spouses, because they breed politics. Whenever two of our people get married, one of them must depart—preferably the female, to look after her baby.

Savvy Leadership

Do not summon subordinates to your office, Ogilvy advised, because it scares them. Go to their office; it puts them at ease and makes you more visible throughout the organization.

---

4. I admire people who work with gusto. If you don't enjoy what you are doing, I beg you to find another job. Remember the Scottish proverb, "Be happy while you're living, for you're a long time dead."

5. I despise toadies who suck up to their bosses; they are generally the same people who bully their subordinates.

6. I admire self-confident professionals, the craftsmen who do their jobs with superlative excellence. They always seem to respect the expertise of their colleagues. They don't poach.

7. I admire people who hire subordinates who are good enough to succeed them. I pity people who are so insecure that they feel compelled to hire inferiors as their subordinates.

8. I admire people who build up their subordinates, because this is the only way we can promote from within the ranks.

I detest having to go outside to fill important jobs, and I look forward to the day when that will never be necessary.

9. I admire people with gentle manners who treat other people as human beings. I abhor quarrelsome people. I abhor people who wage paper-warfare. The best way to keep the peace is to be candid. Remember Blake:

> I was angry with my friend;
> I told my wrath, my wrath did end.
> I was angry with my foe;
> I told it not, my wrath did grow.

10. I admire well-organized people who deliver their work on time. The Duke of Wellington never went home until he had finished *all* the work on his desk.

What I Expect of Myself

Having told my staff what I expect of them, I then tell them what I expect of myself:

1. I try to be fair and to be firm, to make unpopular decisions without cowardice, to create an atmosphere of stability, and to listen more than I talk.
2. I try to sustain the momentum of the agency—its ferment, its vitality, its forward thrust.
3. I try to build the agency by landing new accounts. (At this point the upturned faces in my audience look like baby birds waiting for the father bird to feed them.)

(Continued)

4. I try to win the confidence of our clients at their highest level.
5. I try to make sufficient profits to keep you all from penury in old age.
6. I plan our policies far into the future.
7. I try to recruit people of the highest quality at all levels, to build the hottest staff in the agency business.
8. I try to get the best out of every man and woman in the agency.

Andrew Carnegie

1835–1919

*S*cottish-born Andrew Carnegie immigrated to the United States in 1848 and, in the classic rags-to-riches story, became the king of steel. His first job was in a textile factory earning $1.20 a week. At 16, he became a telegraph operator for the Pennsylvania Railroad, where his boss showed him the ropes of business and investing. Carnegie struck out on his own in 1865, selling bonds, building bridges, and managing an iron ore foundry; then, in 1873 he started to focus on steel. Unfortunately, the Homestead Steel Worker's strike of 1892, in which 10 men were killed and scores were injured, has left a black mark on his legacy. On the other hand, Carnegie was considered a saint for giving more than $325 million to public causes.

The Road to Business Success

- The rising man must do something exceptional, and beyond the range of his special department. HE MUST ATTRACT ATTENTION.
- Always break orders to save owners. There never was a great character who did not sometimes smash the routine regulations and make new ones for himself.

- Boss your boss just as soon as you can; try it on early. There is nothing he will like so well if he is the right kind of boss; if he is not, he is not the man for you to remain with—leave him whenever you can, even at a present sacrafice, and find one capable of discerning genius.

- There is always a boom in brains, cultivate that crop, for if you grow any amount of that commodity, here is your best market and you cannot overstock it, and the more brains you have to sell, the higher price you can exact.

- And here is the prime condition for success, the great secret: concentrate your energy, thought, and capital exclusively upon the business in which you are engaged. . . . I tell you "put all your eggs in one basket, and then watch that basket."

Outrageous Promotion

With great hoopla, Carnegie named his first steel plant after his most important customer— Edgar Thomson, president of the Pennsylvania Railroad.

Savvy Leadership

According to one of Carnegie's lieutenants, the steel king advised that you should never "blame your men for little, trivial faults. If you do, you will dishearten them." If criticism was necessary, Carnegie never did so in front of others.

John H. Johnson

1918–

*J*ohn Johnson, *founder of* Negro Digest, Ebony, *and* Fashion Fair Cosmetics, *among many other ventures, is the most powerful African-American businessperson in the United States. Not bad, considering his father was killed when Johnson was just a child and he then grew up in poverty. To inspire himself as a young man, he made a habit of reading Dale Carnegie's* How to Win Friends and Influence People *in high school. In 1942, he founded* Negro Digest *by putting his mother's furniture up as collateral for a $500 loan; in 1945, he founded* Ebony *magazine, the cornerstone of his empire. In breaking through racial barriers to attract advertising from white-owned companies, Johnson often had less than five minutes to say his piece.*

How to Sell Anything in Five Minutes or Less

Whether I had five or thirty-five minutes, I always based my presentation on three tried-and-tested rules:

1. Grab the client's attention in the first two or three seconds with a fact or an emotional statement that hits him where he lives or does business.

2. Find the vulnerable spot. Everybody has something that will make him or her move or say yes. It may have nothing in the world to do with his or her business life. It may be a dream or a hope or a commitment to a person or a thing. Selling is finding the vulnerable point and pushing the yes button.

Smart Habits

To inspire a positive mental attitude, Johnson would lock himself in his office and say the word *success* over and over.

A remarkable example of this was reported by William Grayson, who discovered that a powerful advertising executive was a fan of Roy Campanella, the great Brooklyn Dodgers catcher. The executive and his son virtually lived in the old Ebbets Field and virtually worshipped the home-plate ground Campanella walked on.

Extreme Measures

Early on as an entrepreneur, Johnson so feared failure that he fired an employee merely for suggesting that Johnson might fail.

Grayson, who lived down the street from Campanella, asked the baseball star to autograph one of his home-run balls to the boy. The ball carried not only Campanella's name but the date he hit the home run. By coincidence, the advertising executive and his son had been in Ebbets Field on the day Campanella hit the home run. That sold the account. Nothing—neither statistics nor pretty graphs nor hundreds of telephone calls—was as powerful as an unexpectedly powerful gift to a loved one.

3. Find and emphasize common ground. You and the client may disagree on many things. You may like Jesse Jackson and he or she may dislike Jesse Jackson. You're not there to

talk about what divides you. You're there to emphasize the values, hopes, and aspirations that bind you together. Successful selling is a matter of finding common ground, no matter how narrow it might be, on which you and your client can stand together.

Jo Foxworth

*W*hen Jo Foxworth, who founded her own advertising agency, was inducted into the American Advertising Hall of Fame in 1997, she was one of only six women to have received the honor. And to think that she was thrown out of Mississippi State College for Women for protesting a curriculum designed to make wives out of them. Foxworth earned a degree in journalism from the University of Missouri, and then went to work for a newspaper—selling advertising. For a number of years, she worked in the advertising departments of various stores. Eventually, Foxworth joined the McCann-Erickson advertising agency as a copywriter in 1955. After successful work on campaigns for companies such as Westinghouse, Procter & Gamble, and Coca-Cola, Foxworth, who espouses listening to your customer, founded her own firm in 1968.

Shut Up and Listen

Although the sound of one's own voice may be the sweetest music this side of Lincoln Center, the world and our own little plots of it in particular would probably be better if we'd shut up and listen more often. It boils down to this:

1. *Silence IS golden, no matter what they say at CBS and your friendly local disco.* As noise pollution rises, so does the premium on quiet. Please do not disturb the peace at the office any more than it is disturbed already.
2. *While "thinking out loud" may help you crystallize your own ideas, this may also keep other people from crystallizing theirs.* Since theirs can do you as much good as your own—maybe even more than yours—make your conversation an exchange, not a monologue.
3. *Do not let people outside your organization pick your brains unless they're good friends—or willing to pay.* What you know is worth money. Why give it away for the sake of a little ego trip?

> **Savvy Leadership**
> Don't overdecorate your office, she advises, because you want people to pay attention to you, not what's on the wall.

4. *Don't speak up at a meeting until you have something meaningful to contribute.* Talking to attract attention may call attention only to your blank spots.
5. *Do not interrupt busy or worried people with gratuitous advice and comment.* Do not present them with any problem or idea that can wait.
6. *Never, never under any circumstances talk when you don't know what you're talking about.* This is the most obvious dictum in business, yet it remains the one most often violated.
7. *When you do speak, control the volume.* The female voice under stress can be an extremely unpleasant sound. It's hard to remember this when you're angry, upset or excited, but try to keep your voice down.

Questions about Age, Salary, and Sex

In the immortal words of Casey Stengel, you don't have to tell nobody nuttin'. Practice smiling. And remember that an unanswered question is stickier for the asker than the askee. Keep the following points in mind:

1. *Don't tell your age to anybody.* You may be so proud of being the youngest executive in the history of the company that you'll be tempted to shout it from the air-conditioning tower, but you'll be another middle-aged executive someday and maybe not so eager to broadcast it.
2. *Don't tell your salary to anybody.* This is privileged information, and spreading it around can cause trouble to top management. Top managements hate trouble, and one of the first things you learn when you're running a company is why they're such bastards up there.
3. *Don't tell the fascinating story of your sex life to anybody.* Now that everybody's lurid sexual exploits are in the public domain, you can't impress your associates with yours anyway, and Mr. Omnipotence and his wife may be a pair of gold-seal prudes.

Theodore N. Vail

1845–1920

*A*lthough Alexander Graham Bell patented the telephone in 1876, it was Theodore Vail who pioneered the building of the infrastructure for the telephone. Vail, who was working for the U.S. Railway Service and was considered the foremost expert in mail delivery, was hired by Bell Telephone in 1878. His mission was to take on Western Union and replace the telegraph with the telephone as the most important device for communication. Implicit in this mission was the job of networking the country with telephone lines, just as Vail had done with his system for mail delivery. In 1880, Vail won his battle with Western Union when he convinced them to sell out their interests, and in 1885, Bell formally became American Telephone and Telegraph. As a pioneer, Vail knew all too well the importance of decisiveness and perseverance when it comes to success.

The Making of a Businessman

In the making of a businessman, and in the course of a business life, there are practices to be cultivated, things to be learned and habits to be formed that are most helpful to success. These are the most important of them:

Extreme Measures

Vail insisted that senior managers meet him on his yacht; he did not let them off until particular problems were solved or policies were agreed to.

- Concentration upon and application to the work in hand, to the exclusion, for the time being, of all other work.
- Definiteness of purpose and thoroughness in deciding on a pursuit, and in doing and learning all that is necessary to be done or known for its accomplishment.
- Observation, or the habit of noticing little things—instinctive recognition of anything wrong, or out of place. This is incidental to orderly habits, or the result of them. General deductions from single incidents should never be made. One incident may be accidental; many similar incidents come from a common cause.
- Foresight and precaution; there never was a successful leader who did not continue all precautions until the moment of success.
- Self-confidence, without overconfidence or offensive egotism; it should rest on a thorough knowledge of what is to be done, or on experience in the doing, or on both.
- Respect for the unknown; in every undertaking there are difficulties that only a familiar and practical acquaintance can reveal.
- Respect for the opinions of others.
- Deliberation over new ideas. Many thoughts that are seemingly wonderful lose their apparent value when slept over, or exposed to impartial criticism.
- Attention without interruption to anyone who is at all entitled to be heard. Cultivate the mind in many directions. To

know intelligently about many things is always valuable to a business man.

• Reciprocity in all the affairs of life. It is only by reciprocity that permanent success can be gained. Every exchange should benefit both sides.

Those who feel discouraged by hard conditions should remember that most successful men have started under discouraging conditions.

Henry Ford II
1917–1987

*F*illing the shoes of legendary Henry Ford was a herculean task, but Henry Ford II had little choice when his senile grandfather started running the Ford Motor Company into the ground in the 1940s. No one thought that young Ford would amount to much, but he enlisted in the Navy during World War II against the family's wishes to prove his independence and his worth. When his father Edsel Ford died in 1943, Henry II was permitted to leave the Navy to help run the car company, which needed a serious housecleaning. Even then, however, it took two years before he was made president. Henry II, who knew what he wanted in an employee and hired the best, is credited with turning around the company in the postwar years, and the famous Mustang was introduced during his watch in 1964.

What an Employer Wants

In considering a man for a management job or for other work, every employer must ask himself, "Would this applicant, if hired, be an asset to my company?" We know many of the qualities that make a man an asset to a business. Here are the main ones.

- *Proficiency in your field.* Your college training is the company's justification for hiring you. But you should remember that when an employer thinks about an applicant's college training, he thinks about more than a major in one field. He thinks about the applicant's reading speed and comprehension; his ability to write the English language and his knowledge of the principles of mathematics. These form the hard logical base not only of a successful education but of a successful career as well. Naturally, the better prepared you are in accounting or public relations, engineering or market research, product design or law, the better are your chances of matching the description of the job that is open. Never forget, however, that specialized training alone is not enough. It may get you that first job; but if it is all you have to offer an employer, it may also bury you in that first job.

> ### Smart Habits
> Henry Ford II insisted on complete order in his life; for example, he cataloged every single personal possession of consequence.

- *Social competence.* This is the kind of unsatisfactory term that always means too many things. Perhaps I can clarify it somewhat by pointing out that the social skills a young man learns while in school will serve him well in a large corporation. The ability to cooperate with others in purposeful activity, congeniality, knowing how to follow and lead—all of these personal traits are important in school, and they are important in a company. I don't mean to suggest that an employer is going to be impressed automatically by a long list of extracurricular activities. Your chairmanship of the dance committee speaks highly for you. But for an employer, your chairmanships in the professional and honorary societies speak more highly—and more to the point. They indicate that you possess the kinds of skills which are highly prized in a company.

- *Analytical power.* You exercise this power in the classroom to the extent that you gather evidence, interpret it and draw logical conclusions. You will also exercise it in business, but there will be a difference—a big one. When you apply the scientific method to a problem in a classroom, usually you don't apply all of it. In a mathematics class, for example, a teacher gives you the problem, and you work out the solution to it. In business, you often have to find the problem before you can even start thinking about the solution. In business, recognizing the problem is just as important as knowing the method that will solve it.

Extreme Measures

Back in the 1940s, when Henry Ford II was reorganizing the Ford Motor Company and purging dubious individuals, he took to packing a gun to protect himself against reprisals.

- *Curiosity.* An employer is always on the lookout for questing minds. Many people with specialized training and the ability to reason can deal easily with accepted facts. Fewer people are blessed with the kind of curiosity that breaks up familiar patterns and starts fresh thoughts. This is the very source of innovation—the less costly manufacturing technique, the quicker accounting system, the more effective sales plan, the better design.
- *Integrity.* This is the quality that gives meaning to all the rest. You must have it first of all for yourself, of course, for without

it no person is whole. But individual integrity also makes group integrity and this is essential to a company. It is the guidance-and-control system that directs company performance. And by its performance over the long haul, a company lives or dies.

Andrew S. Grove
1936–

*I*ntel's chairman, Andrew Grove, made famous the motto, "Only the paranoid survive"—a philosophy developed and necessary in his youth. Life was more than a challenge growing up Jewish in Hungary; during World War II, his father was taken to a labor camp, and his mother and he survived the Nazi occupation by obtaining false papers. When the Soviets invaded Hungary in 1956, Grove chose to escape to the United States. After earning a Ph.D. in chemical engineering from the University of California, Berkeley, Grove went to work for Fairchild Semiconductor, where he met the future founders of Intel, Gordon Moore and Robert Noyce. Grove, who has managed his career by continually asking himself how to add value, joined them at Intel in 1968 and became president in 1979. He later added the titles of CEO and chairman.

Managing Your Own Career

As a general rule, you have to accept that no matter where you work, you are not an employee; you are in a business with one employee—yourself. You are in competition with millions of similar businesses, millions of others all over the world, picking up the pace, capable of doing the same work that you can do and perhaps more eager.

The point is, the cliches of globalization and the information revolution have real meaning—potentially deadly meaning—for your career. The sad news is, nobody owes you a career. You own it as a sole proprietor. I can offer you no sure-fire formula for success. But here are three key questions:

Savvy Leadership

To remain accessible to all employees, Grove works in an 8-foot by 9-foot cubicle.

1. Continually ask, Am I adding real value or merely passing information along? How do you add more value? By continually looking for ways to make things truly better in your organization. In principle, every hour of your day should be spent increasing the output or the value of the output of the people for whom you're responsible.
2. Continually ask, Am I plugged into what's happening around me? Inside the company? The industry? Are you a node connected to a network of plugged-in people or are you floating by yourself?
3. Are you trying new ideas, new techniques, and new technologies?—and I mean personally. Don't just read about them.

Smart Habits

To gather poignant information from others in an efficient manner, Grove recommends doing so by phone or through a quick exchange by just poking your head in their office/cubicle. Scheduled information-sharing meetings involve too much social etiquette and waste time.

People do not always face up to changes they have to deal with, yet you can't be ready for the future until you've survived the crucible of change. And the key to survival is to learn to add more value today, and every day.

Strategic Inflection Points

Major change in the competitive landscape can take many forms. It may be the introduction of new technologies, a new regulatory environment, or a sudden shift in customer preferences. But the change usually hits the organization in such a way that those of us in senior management are among the last to notice.

Such monumental changes represent what I call Strategic Inflection Points — events that cause you to fundamentally change your business strategy. At such moments in the life of an organization, nothing less will do.

The biggest difficulty with Strategic Inflection Points — aside from the havoc they create — is distinguishing them from the many changes that routinely impinge on your business. Obviously, not every change we respond to requires a dramatic reaction. But the answers to three questions may signal the onset of such a change:

- *Has the company of the entity that you most worry about shifted?* I have a mental "silver bullet" test. If you had one bullet, what would you shoot with it? If you change the direction of the gun, that is one of the signals that you may be dealing with something more than an ordinary shift in the competitive landscape.
- *Is your key complementor — a company whose work you rely on to make your product more available — changing?*

A shift in direction by a partner or market ally can be as decisive as a move by a competitor.

- *Do the people you have worked with for 20 years seem to be talking gibberish?* Are they suddenly talking about people, products, or companies that no one had heard of a year before? If so, it's time to pay attention to what's going on.

PART IV

~

Wall Street Wizards

Warren E. Buffett

1930–

*T*he billionaire investor was said to have discovered money like "Mozart discovered music." Imagine: $10,000 invested with Warren Buffett in 1956 was worth $80 million in 1994. He has always worked hard; as a kid he had two paper routes, retrieved golf balls for resale, and managed pinball machines. After attending the University of Nebraska, he studied at Columbia University, where he met his mentor Benjamin Graham, the undisputed father of modern securities analysis. In 1956, Buffett started his own investing firm and then bought Berkshire Hathaway, turning it into a holding company for his investments. He made a killing by investing in companies with virtual monopolies in their industries such as Coca-Cola, Disney, and Gilette.

Investment Principles

- Rule No. 1: Never lose money. Rule No. 2: Never forget Rule No. 1.
- I never attempt to make money on the stock market. I buy on the assumption that they could close the market the next day and not reopen it for five years.
- The market is there only as a reference point to see if anybody is offering anything foolish. When we invest in stocks, we invest in businesses.

- The dumbest reason to buy a stock is because it's going up.
- Great investment opportunities come around when excellent companies are surrounded by unusual circumstances that cause the stock to be misappraised.
- We don't make judgments based on ratings. If we wanted Moody's and Standard & Poor's to run our money, we'd give it to them.

Extreme Measures

When Buffett is asked how long he holds a stock, he answers, "My favorite time frame for holding a stock is forever." For example, he's owned Disney for more than 30 years.

- Draw a circle around the businesses you understand and then eliminate those that fail to qualify on the basis of value, good management, and limited exposure to hard times.
- I can't be involved in 50 or 75 things. That's a Noah's Ark way of investing—you end up with a zoo that way. I like to put meaningful amounts of money in a few things.
- I read annual reports of the company I'm looking at and I read the annual reports of the competitors—that is the main source of material.
- We love the kinds of companies that can do well in international markets, obviously, particularly where they're largely untapped.
- You should invest in a business that even a fool can run, because someday a fool will.

Sir John M. Templeton

S ir John Templeton was a master at discovering international investment opportunities long before it became fashionable. For example, by the mid-1960s, Templeton and his venerable Templeton Funds were invested in Japan, where stocks were trading at 4 times earnings, whereas U.S. stocks were at 16. "To get a bargain price, you've got to look for where the public is most frightened and pessimistic," he said. Templeton was intrigued by foreign lands while growing up in rural Tennessee, and was so captivated by stories told by visiting Christian missionaries, he thought of becoming one. However, after attending Yale and Oxford as a Rhodes scholar, he realized his real forte was with money and finding great investments where others feared to tread.

The Time-Tested Maxims of the Templeton Touch

1. For all long-term investors, there is only one objective— "maximum total real return after taxes."
2. Achieving a good record takes much study and work, and is a lot harder than most people think.
3. It is impossible to produce a superior performance unless you do something different from the majority.

4. The time of maximum pessimism is the best time to buy, and the time of maximum optimism is the best time to sell.

5. To put "Maxim 4" in somewhat different terms, in the stock market the only way to get a bargain is to buy what most investors are selling.

6. To buy when others are despondently selling and to sell when others are greedily buying requires the greatest fortitude, even while offering the greatest reward.

7. Bear markets have always been temporary. Share prices turn upward from one to twelve months before the bottom of the business cycle.

8. If a particular industry or type of security becomes popular with investors, that popularity will always prove temporary and, when lost, won't return for many years.

9. In the long run, the stock market indexes fluctuate around the long-term upward trend of earnings per share.

10. In free-enterprise nations, the earnings on stock market indexes fluctuate around the replacement book value of the shares of the index.

11. If you buy the same securities as other people, you will have the same results as other people.

12. The time to buy a stock is when the short-term owners have finished their selling, and the time to sell a stock is often when short-term owners have finished their buying.

13. Share prices fluctuate much more widely than values. Therefore, index funds will never produce the best total return performance.

14. Too many investors focus on "outlook" and "trends." Therefore, more profit is made by focusing on value.

15. If you search worldwide, you will find more bargains and better bargains than by studying only one nation. Also, you gain the safety of diversification.

16. The fluctuation of share prices is roughly proportional to the square root of the price.

17. The time to sell an asset is when you have found a much better bargain to replace it.

18. When any method for selecting stocks becomes popular, then switch to unpopular methods. As has been suggested in "Maxim 3," too many investors can spoil any share-selection method or any market-timing formula.

Savvy Leadership

For some 30 years, Templeton led the Templeton Growth Fund directors in prayer at their meetings, that is, praying they make smart investments. Prayer, he believed, enabled them to think more clearly.

19. Never adopt permanently any type of asset or any selection method. Try to stay flexible, open-minded and skeptical. Long-term top results are achieved only by changing from popular to unpopular the types of securities you favor and your methods of selection.

20. The skill factor in selection is largest for the common-stock part of your investments.

21. The best performance is produced by a person, not a committee.

22. If you begin with prayer, you can think more clearly and make fewer stupid mistakes.

Bernard M. Baruch

1870–1965

As a boy, future Wall Street powerhouse Bernard Baruch picked cotton to earn money for powder and shot so he could hunt rabbits. He grew up in rural South Carolina, where whites and blacks clashed constantly, eventually prompting the family to move to New York City. After attending City College, Baruch went to Colorado in search of adventure and gold, but in 1891, he was back in New York, working as a clerk and then an analyst for an investing firm. Not long after, he struck out on his own, raising money from others to invest. Baruch, who moved in the right circles (e.g., the Rockefellers and the Guggenheims), made millions in the stock market with some help from his powerful friends. His key to success was employing a skeptical philosophy that was focused on separating facts from emotion.

My Investment Philosophy

Being so skeptical about the usefulness of advice, I have been reluctant to lay down any "rules" or guidelines on how to invest or speculate wisely. Still, there are a number of things I have learned from my own experience which might be worth listing for those who are able to muster the necessary self-discipline:

1. Don't speculate unless you can make it a full-time job.
2. Beware of barbers, beauticians, waiters—of anyone—bringing gifts of "inside" information or "tips."
3. Before you buy a security, find out everything you can about the company, its management and competitors, its earnings and possibilities for growth.
4. Don't try to buy at the bottom and sell at the top. This can't be done—except by liars.
5. Learn how to take your losses quickly and cleanly. Don't expect to be right all the time. If you have made a mistake, cut your losses as quickly as possible.
6. Don't buy too many different securities. Better have only a few investments which can be watched.

Smart Habits

Although hard to stomach, Baruch always analyzed his losses to determine his mistake(s). To do so, he would break away from Wall Street and find a quiet place to review what he'd done. The review always included a period of self-examination to understand his own failings.

---

7. Make a periodic reappraisal of all your investments to see whether changing developments have altered their prospects.
8. Study your tax position to know when you can sell to greatest advantage.
9. Always keep a good part of your capital in a cash reserve. Never invest all your funds.
10. Don't try to be a jack of all investments. Stick to the field you know best.

These "rules" mainly reflect two lessons that experience has taught me—that getting the facts of a situation before acting is of crucial importance, and that getting these facts is a continuous job which requires eternal vigilance.

Two Principal Mistakes

There are two principal mistakes that nearly all amateurs in the stock market make.

The first is to have an inexact knowledge of the securities in which one is dealing, to know too little about a company's management, its earnings and prospects for future growth.

The second mistake is to trade beyond one's financial resources, to try to run up a fortune on a shoestring. That was my main error at the outset. I had virtually no "capital" to start with. When I bought stocks I put up so small a margin that a change of a few points would wipe out my equity. What I really was doing was little more than betting whether a stock would go up or down. I might be right sometimes, but any sizable fluctuation would wipe me out.

John C. Bogle
1929–

J ohn Bogle founded The Vanguard Group, a highly successful
*family of mutual funds, in 1974. After attending Princeton
University, where he wrote his senior thesis on mutual funds,
Bogle joined a Wall Street firm and worked with such drive that
he suffered a heart attack at age 30. Not to be thwarted, he
became a pioneer in creating index funds. A key factor in his success was keeping management costs to a minimum, relying heavily on computers for analysis and transactions — the average cost
of the company's funds have been less than one-third of the
industry average. Before Bogle retired in 1996 (after a heart
transplant), he could boast that the size of his group's assets were
second only to Fidelity, a monumental achievement built upon
his 12 pillars of wisdom that espouse simplicity.*

Twelve Pillars of Wisdom

1. *Investing is not nearly as difficult as it looks.* The intelligent investor in mutual funds, using common sense and
   without extraordinary financial acumen, can perform with
   the pros. In a world where financial markets are highly
   efficient, there is absolutely no reason that careful and disciplined novices — those who know the rudiments but lack

the experience—cannot hold their own or even surpass the long-term returns earned by professional investors as a group. Successful investing involves doing just a few things right and avoiding serious mistakes.

2. *When all else fails, fall back on simplicity.* If you have a major investment decision to make, there are an infinite number of solutions that would be worse than this one: commit, over a period of a few years, half of your assets to a stock index fund and half to a bond index fund. Ignore interim fluctuations in their net asset values. Hold your positions for as long as you live, subject only to infrequent and marginal adjustments as your circumstances change. Occam's razor—a thesis set forth 600 years ago and often affirmed by experience since then—should encourage you: when there are multiple solutions to a problem, choose the simplest one.

3. *Time marches on.* Time dramatically enhances capital accumulation as the magic of compounding accelerates. At an annual return of +10%, the additional capital accumulation on a $10,000 investment is $1,000 in the first year, $2,400 by the tenth year, and $10,000 by the twenty-fifth year. At the end of 25 years, the total value of the initial $10,000 investment is $108,000, nearly a tenfold increase in value. Give yourself the benefit of all the time you can possibly afford.

4. *Nothing ventured, nothing gained.* It pays to take reasonable interim risks in the search for higher long-term rates of return. The magic of compounding accelerates sharply with even modest increases in annual rate of return. While an investment of $10,000 earning an annual return of +10%

grows to a value of $108,000 over 25 years, at +12% the final value is $170,000. The difference of $62,000 is more than six times the initial investment itself.

5. *Diversify, diversify, diversify.* It is hard to imagine that a principle as basic as investment diversification can be so valuable. By investing in mutual funds you can eliminate the risk of owning the stock or bond of a single enterprise that may deteriorate and never fully recover, or even fail altogether. The passage of time has no impact on this specific security risk. By owning a broadly diversified portfolio of stocks and bonds, only market risk remains. This risk is reflected in the volatility of the total value of your portfolio and should take care of itself over time as reinvested dividends and interest are compounded.

6. *The eternal triangle.* Never forget that risk, return, and cost are the three sides of the eternal triangle of investing. Remember also that the cost penalty may sharply erode the risk premium to which an investor is entitled. This is not to say that you should necessarily seek out the lowest-cost mutual fund option. Rather, you should understand unequivocally that investing in a fund with a relatively high expense ratio—more than 0.50% per year for a money market fund, 0.75% for a bond fund, 1.00% for a regular equity fund, or 0.30% for an index fund—bears careful examination. Unless you are confident that the higher costs you incur are justified by higher expected returns or enhanced value of service, select your investments from among the lower-cost no-load funds.

7. *The powerful magnetism of the mean.* In the world of investing, the mean is a powerful magnet that pulls financial mar-

The eternal triangle of investing.

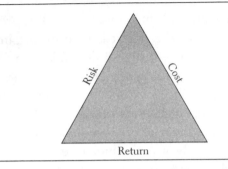

ket returns toward it, causing returns to deteriorate after
they exceed historical norms by substantial margins and to
improve after they fall short. The mean is also the powerful
magnet that pulls the returns achieved by portfolio managers toward it, causing a fund's return to move, over time,
ever closer to the average returns achieved by other funds.
Regression to the mean is a manifestation of the immutable
law of averages that prevails, sooner or later, in the financial
jungle.

8. *Do not overestimate your ability to pick superior equity mutual
    funds, nor underestimate your ability to pick superior bond and
    money market funds.* In selecting equity funds, no analysis of
    the past, no matter how painstaking, assures future superior-
    ity. In general, you should settle for a solid mainstream equity
    fund in which the action of the stock market itself explains
    about 85% or more of the fund's return. Combining several
    low-cost equity funds to achieve this diversification is equally
    sensible; so is the holding of a single low-cost index fund. But
    do not approach the selection of bond and money market
    funds with the same skepticism. Selecting the better funds in

these categories on the basis of their comparative costs holds remarkably favorable prospects for success.

9. *You may have a stable principal value or a stable income stream, but you may not have both.* Nothing could make this proposition more obvious than the contrast between a 90-day U.S. Treasury bill—with its volatile income stream and fixed value—and a 30-year U.S. Treasury bond—with its fixed income stream and extraordinarily volatile market value. Intelligent investing involves choices, compromises, and trade-offs, and your own financial position should determine which type of stability—or, more likely, which combination of the two—is most suitable for your portfolio.

10. *Beware of "fighting the last war."* Too many investors—individuals and institutions alike—are constantly making investment decisions based on the lessons of the recent, or even the extended, past. They seek stocks after stocks have emerged victorious from the last war, bonds after bonds have won, Treasury bills after bills have won. And they worry about the impact of inflation *after* inflation, having turned high real returns into so-so nominal returns, has become the accepted bogeyman. You should not ignore the past, but neither should you assume that a particular cyclical trend will last forever. None does.

Savvy Leadership

Although Bogle founded a mutual fund company, he advises investors to beware of "past performance syndrome" in mutual fund advertising. In other words, beware of those who claim that their fund is No. 1. Why? First, hundreds of funds can claim that they're No. 1 based on select criteria, and second, the chances of a fund repeating as a No. 1 performer in the near future is essentially zero, according to Bogle.

11. *You rarely, if ever, know something the market does not.* It is really not possible to do so. If you are worried about the coming bear market, excited about the coming bull market, fearful about the prospect of war, or concerned about the economy, the election, or indeed the state of mankind, in all probability your opinions are already reflected in the market. The financial markets reflect the knowledge, the hopes, the fears, even the greed, of all investors everywhere. It is nearly always unwise to act on insights that you think are your own but are in fact shared by millions of others.

12. *Think long term.* Do not let transitory changes in stock prices alter your investment program. There is a lot of noise in the daily volatility of the stock market, which too often is "a tale told by an idiot, full of sound and fury, signifying nothing." (Macbeth would doubtless agree.) Stocks may remain overvalued, or undervalued, for years. Patience and consistency are valuable assets for the intelligent investor. The best rule is: stay the course.

Caveat Emptor: The Best-Laid Schemes

There are intelligent ways to go about investing and less intelligent ways. Although the odds are heavily against them, some foolish investors are ever seeking to grow rich, using Dr. Johnson's words, "beyond the dreams of avarice." In the real world of investing, such dreams rarely become reality. But even pursuing the sensible, time-honored policies of conservative investing is no guarantee of financial enrichment. The most intelligent of plans often go awry. As Robert Burns warned, "the best laid schemes of mice and men gang aft a-gley." So know yourself, educate yourself, determine for yourself the financial plan best suited to your own objectives, and have the wisdom, patience, and emotional discipline to stay the course that you have chosen. Finally, make your own careful judgments about all of the investment advice that you receive—including, dare I say, even the well-intentioned and experienced advice provided in this book.

Philip L. Carret
1896–1998

*W*arren Buffett declares that if there were ever a hall of fame for investment advisers, Philip Carret would be among the first inducted. Carret studied chemistry at Harvard and then trained as an aviator for World War I, but didn't see action. Afterward, he sold bonds, but then quit to become a reporter for Barron's. While there, he came up with the idea of pooling various individual's money for investment and left to found one of the first mutual funds, the Pioneer Fund, in 1928. Carret managed the fund until 1963, when he sold it and founded Carret and Co., a money management company. At the age of 101, he was still going to the office and forever remained cynical in evaluating companies, a trait that Carret believed went a long way when it comes to successful investing.

Twelve Commandments for Speculators

1. Never hold fewer than ten different securities covering five different fields of business.
2. At least once in six months reappraise every security held.
3. Keep at least half the total fund in income-producing securities.

4. Consider yield the least important factor in analyzing any stock.
5. Be quick to take losses, reluctant to take profits.
6. Never put more than 25% of a given fund into securities about which detailed information is not readily and regularly available.
7. Avoid "inside information" as you would the plague.
8. Seek facts diligently, advice never.
9. Ignore mechanical formulas for valuing securities.
10. When stocks are high, money rates rising, business prosperous, at least half a given fund should be placed in short-term bonds.
11. Borrow money sparingly and only when stocks are low, money rates low or falling, and business depressed.
12. Set aside a moderate proportion of available funds for the purchase of long-term options on stocks of promising companies whenever available.

Smart Habits

Carret always searched his immediate surroundings for investment ideas; for example, he used Neutrogena soap while staying in a Boston hotel, was impressed, and bought the stock. Years later, Johnson & Johnson was equally impressed and bought Neutrogena; Carret made a killing.

Smart Habits

Once you buy a stock, evaluate your holding once every six months. If you do so more frequently, Carret warned, you're more likely to sell it sooner than you should or churn your portfolio. It could take years for a stock price to reflect the value of the company.

Charles Schwab

*M*oney *magazine selected Charles Schwab, who has built a discount brokerage powerhouse, as one of seven people who most influences the economy. After receiving an MBA from Stanford University, Schwab entered the investment world in 1957. He was working for a small California investment adviser when he and two partners decided to start their own mutual fund company in 1971. Unfortunately, they failed to properly register with securities regulators and were closed down. Schwab went on to found Charles Schwab & Co. in 1974. Nine years later, he sold a controlling interest to BankAmerica to raise money for expansion, but then bought it back in 1987 and took the firm public that same year. Whether you be a novice or an experienced investor looking for diversity, he believes in a basic checklist for picking mutual funds.*

The Bottom Line on Mutual Funds

- To be a successful investor, you don't have to outperform the market; you only have to match it.
- I consider mutual funds to be the investment of choice for many of us. With one investment, you get diversification that might otherwise be impossible.

- No-load mutual funds are about the best investment you can make for an IRA.
- Index funds can be a great way to invest, for both first-time and experienced investors.
- Consider only funds that are listed in reputable financial publications.
- Consider only no-load mutual funds.
- Look for funds that have good performance records, not only for this year but over the life of the fund.
- A good way to diversify is to use a "core and explore" approach. You use index funds to form the core of your portfolio and selectively add actively managed funds for further diversification or to try to beat the market.

> ### *Smart Habits*
> As you follow the stock market, don't overindulge in your reading and research. Schwab prefers the *Wall Street Journal* as his daily paper and finds *Forbes* and *Money* to be the best magazines. While reading, pay attention to the advertisements—there might be an investing opportunity behind an ad.

- Unless you're an experienced investor, avoid sector funds.
- The best source I know of for timely fund information is the Internet.
- With mutual funds, as with other investments, the higher the risk, the greater the potential reward.
- Taxes can have a huge impact on mutual fund returns. Check the investment philosophy or strategy defined in the fund's prospectus. An investment that is suitable for a tax-deferred account (such as an IRA) may not be as appropriate for a taxable account.
- It's my feeling that international investing is a key part of asset allocation, and that every portfolio should include an international component.

Henry Clews
1834–1923

*H*enry Clews was once a powerful figure on the Street and
wrote several insightful books on the subject (often
quoted by historians). While growing up in England, his parents expected him to join the family business of manufacturing
china. However, when he accompanied his father to New York
City in 1850, Clews became enthralled with the American
lifestyle and never returned. He found a clerk position with a
large importer and then moved into finance. Before long, he
and some friends opened a private bank on Wall Street. Ever
ambitious, Clews joined the New York Stock Exchange and
survived battles with such notorious characters as Daniel Drew
and Jay Gould, who ultimately taught him what kind of person
to avoid on Wall Street.

The Study of the Stock Market

Next to the unwisdom of selecting and following bad or incompetent advisers in matters of speculation and investment, there
are also certain persons whom, if you wish to do well and make a
fortune honestly, you should be careful to avoid. You will not
always know them by their appearance; in fact, that is often the

worst rule to go by, for they are generally well disguised. It is in
their walk, talk, and conversation that you will find them out,
and, that this be the easier, I have made a collection of their characteristics, as follows:
Avoid a man

Who vilifies his benefactor;
Who unjustly accuses others of bad deeds;
Who never has a good word for anybody;
Who is always prating about his own virtues;
Who, when he drinks, habitually drinks alone;
Who boasts of the superiority of his family;
Who talks religion down-town in connection with his daily busi-
    ness affairs;
Who talks recklessly against the virtue of respectable women;
Who runs in debt with no apparent intention of paying;
Who borrows small sums on his note or check dated ahead;
Who won't work for an honest living;
Who looks down upon those who do;
Who imputes bad motives to those trying to do good;
Who betrays confidence;
Who lies;
Who is honest only for policy's sake;
Who deceives his wife and boasts of it to others;
Who chews tobacco in a public conveyance;
Who gets intoxicated in public places;
Who partakes of hospitality and talks behind his entertainer's
    back;
Who borrows money from a friend and then blackguards the
    lender.

With a population of 80,000,000* people, which this country now has, it is easy to find associates in life without selecting men possessed of any of these characteristics, and life is the better worth living without them.

You will both save and make money by strict observance of this short catalogue of avoidances. You are not called upon to do anything or to risk any money in the exercise of this discretion. It simply consists in letting such people severely alone, and if you have been in the habit of being imposed upon by such characters, you will find your happiness as well as your treasury greatly increased by prudently avoiding them.

Savvy Leadership

When it comes to deciding whether you should handle your own investment portfolio or seek professional guidance, Clews offered this advice: If you need legal help, you see a lawyer, and if you're sick, you see a doctor. Case closed.

---

*U.S. population in 1900, according to Clews.

Peter Lynch
1944–

*F*or his remarkable performance as manager of Fidelity's renowned Magellan Fund, Peter Lynch was named one of the greatest investors of all time by the Wall Street Journal. While growing up in a Boston suburb, he caddied at the local country club for big-shot executives who talked money, and the boy was hooked. Lynch attended Boston College on a caddy scholarship and then went to Wharton. In 1969, he was hired by Fidelity as a research analyst, specializing in the metals industry; in 1974, he was promoted to research director. Three years later, Lynch was handed Magellan, then worth $20 million with 45 stocks in its portfolio. By the time Lynch, who had a definitive checklist in evaluating companies, retired from active duty in 1990, the fund had diversified into more than 1,200 businesses and was worth almost $13 billion.

The Final Checklist

- Understand the nature of the companies you own and the specific reasons for holding the stock. ("It is really going up!" doesn't count.)
- By putting your stocks into categories you'll have a better idea of what to expect from them.

- Big companies have small moves, small companies have big moves.
- Consider the size of a company if you expect it to profit from a specific product.
- Look for small companies that are already profitable and have proven that their concept can be replicated.
- Be suspicious of companies with growth rates of 50 to 100 percent a year.
- Avoid hot stocks in hot industries.
- Distrust diversifications, which usually turn out to be diworse-ifications.
- Long shots almost never pay off.
- It's better to miss the first move in a stock and wait to see if a company's plans are working out.
- People get incredibly valuable fundamental information from their jobs that may not reach the professionals for months or even years.
- Separate all stock tips from the tipper, even if the tipper is very smart, very rich, and his or her last tip went up.
- Some stock tips, especially from an expert in the field, may turn out to be quite valuable. However, people in the paper industry normally give out tips on drug stocks, and people in the health care field never run out of tips on the coming takeovers in the paper industry.
- Invest in simple companies that appear dull, mundane, out of favor, and haven't caught the fancy of Wall Street.
- Moderately fast growers (20 to 25 percent) in nongrowth industries are ideal investments.
- Look for companies with niches.
- When purchasing depressed stocks in troubled companies,

seek out the ones with the superior financial positions and avoid the ones with loads of bank debt.

- Companies that have no debt can't go bankrupt.
- Managerial ability may be important, but it's quite difficult to assess. Base your purchases on the company's prospects, not on the president's resume or speaking ability.
- A lot of money can be made when a troubled company turns around.
- Carefully consider the price-earnings ratio. If the stock is grossly overpriced, even if everything else goes right, you won't make any money.
- Find a story line to follow as a way of monitoring a company's progress.

Smart Habits

Lynch would visit more than 500 companies a year, but some of his best investments were based on his use of a company's product; for example, he bought into Taco Bell after trying and enjoying one of their burritos on a road trip.

- Look for companies that consistently buy back their own shares.
- Study the dividend record of a company over the years and also how its earnings have fared in past recessions.
- Look for companies with little or no institutional ownership.
- All else being equal, favor companies in which management has a significant personal investment over companies run by people that benefit only from their salaries.
- Insider buying is a positive sign, especially when several individuals are buying at once.
- Devote at least an hour a week to investment research. Adding up your dividends and figuring out your gains and losses doesn't count.

- Be patient. Watched stock never boils.
- Buying stocks based on stated book value alone is dangerous and illusory. It's real value that counts.
- When in doubt, tune in later.
- Invest at least as much time and effort in choosing a new stock as you would in choosing a new refrigerator.

PART V

~

Gunslingers and the Entrepreneurial Drive

J. Paul Getty

1892–1976

$\mathcal{J}$. Paul Getty was a master oilman who excelled during the Great Depression and pioneered the drilling of oil in the Middle East in the 1950s; however, his personal life was total chaos as he took lovers across the world, married new wives before he divorced prior ones, and estranged his children in the process. His origins were more humble, growing up a typical child in Minneapolis. His father, an insurance lawyer, was in Oklahoma when the state's first oil was being drilled and he caught the fever, moving the family there and becoming a wildcatter. When Getty graduated college, his father convinced him to join the family's oil business and the young man made his first million in 1916. Getty, who for all his flamboyance took a prudent approach to making his millions, was named the richest man in America by Forbes magazine in 1957.

You Can Make a Million Today

There are no absolutely safe or sure-fire formulas for achieving success in business. Nonetheless, I believe that there are some fundamental rules to the game which, if followed, tip the odds for success very much in the businessman's favor. These are rules which I've applied throughout my entire career—and which every millionaire businessman with whom I am acquainted has followed. The rules have worked for them — and for me. They'll work for you, too.

1. Almost without exception, there is only one way to make a great deal of money in the business world — and that is in one's own business. The man who wants to go into business for himself should choose a field which he knows and understands. Obviously, he can't know everything there is to know from the very beginning, but he should not start until he has acquired a good, solid working knowledge of the business.

2. The businessman should never lose sight of the central aim of all business — to produce more and better goods or provide more and better services to more people at lower cost.

3. A sense of thrift is essential for success in business. The businessman must discipline himself to practice economy wherever possible, in his personal life as well as his business affairs. "Make your money first — then think about spending it," is the best of all possible credos for the man who wishes to succeed.

4. Legitimate opportunities for expansion should never be ignored or overlooked. On the other hand, the businessman must always be on his guard against the temptation to overexpand or launch expansion programs blindly, without sufficient justification and planning. Forced growth can be fatal to any business, new or old.

5. A businessman must run his own business. He cannot expect his employees to think or do as well as he can. If they could, they would not be his employees. When "The Boss" delegates authority or responsibility, he must main-

tain close and constant supervision over the subordinates entrusted with it.

6. The businessman must be constantly alert for new ways to improve his products and services and increase his production and sales. He should also use prosperous periods to find the ways by which techniques may be improved and costs lowered. It is only human for people to give little thought to economies when business is booming. That, however, is just the time when the businessman has the mental elbow room to examine his operations calmly and objectively and thus effect important savings without sacrificing quality or efficiency. Many businessmen wait for lean periods to do these things and, as a result, often hit the panic button and slash costs in the wrong places.

Savvy Leadership

To test the knowledge of his petroleum engineers, Getty would randomly change critical technical data concerning a well site and then see if the engineers noticed.

Extreme Measures

If a roughneck in the oil field questioned Getty's authority (or manhood), Getty challenged him to a treacherous race to the top of an oil rig to settle their differences.

---

7. A businessman must be willing to take risks—to risk his own capital and to use his credit and risk borrowed money as well when, in his considered opinion, the risks are justified. But borrowed money must always be promptly repaid. Nothing will write finis to a career faster than a bad credit rating.

8. A businessman must constantly seek new horizons and untapped or under-exploited markets. As I've already said at some length, most of the world is eager to buy American products and know-how; today's shrewd businessman looks to foreign markets.

9. Nothing builds confidence and volume faster or better than a reputation for standing behind one's work or products. Guarantees should always be honored—and in doubtful cases, the decision should always be in the customer's favor. A generous service policy should also be maintained. The firm that is known to be completely reliable will have little difficulty filling its order books and keeping them filled.

10. No matter how many millions an individual amasses, if he is in business he must always consider his wealth as a means for improving living conditions everywhere. He must remember that he has responsibilities toward his associates, employees, stockholders—and the public.

Do you want to make a million? Believe me, you can—if you are able to recognize the limitless opportunities and potentials around you and will apply these rules and work hard. For today's alert, ambitious and able young men, all that glitters truly *can* be gold.

Dealing with Adversity

1. No matter what happens, do not panic. The panic-stricken individual cannot think or act effectively. A certain amount of trouble is inevitable in any business

career—when it comes, it should be met with calm determination.

2. When things go wrong, it is always a wise idea to pull back temporarily—to withdraw just long enough and far enough to view and evaluate the situation objectively.

3. In the opening stages of any developing adverse situation, it may be necessary and advisable to give some ground, to sacrifice those things which are least important and most expendable. But it should be a fighting withdrawal, a retrograde action that goes back only so far and no further. It must never be a disorderly retreat.

4. Next, all factors in the situation must be examined with meticulous care. Every possible course of action must be weighed. All available resources—cerebral as well as financial, creative as well as practical—must be marshaled.

5. Countermoves must be planned with the greatest care and in the greatest of detail—yet with allowances for alternative courses in the event unforeseen obstacles are encountered. Counteraction must be planned on a scale consistent with the resources available—and the goals set must be conceivably attainable. It is well to bear in mind, however, that the impetus of a properly executed counterattack very often carries the counterattacking force far beyond the point from which it was driven in the first place.

6. Once everything is ready, action should be taken confidently, purposefully, aggressively—and above all, enthusiastically. There can be no hesitation—and it is here that the determination, personality and energy of the leader count the most.

$\mathcal{E}$. W. Scripps built a media empire that included daily newspapers in 15 states, the United Press Association, and the United Feature Syndicate, among other enterprises. He preferred to work from his ranch outside San Diego or from his yacht. His reasons: he was difficult to get along with and he knew it, and to avoid the corruptive nature of wealth and fellow millionaires. "They [millionaires] get to thinking all alike, and their money not only talks, their money does their thinking, too," he said. Ethics was everything to Scripps, who left his empire and the following message to his son: "I would prefer that you should succeed in being in all things a gentleman, according to the real meaning of the word." Although he proclaimed to be an ethical man, his quirky personality and maverick rules for success might lead one to think different.

Some Outlandish Rules for Making Money

1. Never spend as much money as you earn. The smaller your expenditures are in proportion to your earnings the sooner you will become rich.
2. It is more blessed to pay wages than to accept them. At least, it is more profitable.

3. Never do anything yourself that you can get someone else to do for you. The more things that someone else does for you the more time and energy you have to do those things which no one else can do for you.
4. Never do anything today that you can put off till tomorrow. There is always so much to do today that you should not waste your time and energy in doing anything today that can be put off till tomorrow. Most things that you do not have to do today are not worth doing at all.
5. Always buy, never sell. If you've got enough horse sense to become rich you know that it is better to run only one risk than two risks. You also know that just as likely as not the other fellow is smarter than you are and that whether you buy or sell, in each case you run the risk of getting the worst of the bargain. By adopting my rule you will diminish by one-half your chances of loss.
6. Never do anything, if you can help it, that someone else is doing. Why compete with one person or many other persons in any occupation or line of business so long as it is possible for you to have a monopoly in some other field?
7. If circumstances compel you to pursue some occupation or to follow some line of business which is being pursued by some other person, then you do your work in some other way than that in which it is done by the other. There is always a good, better and best way. If you take the best way then the other fellow has no chance of competing with you.
8. Whatever you do once, whatever way you undertake to do a thing, don't do the same thing again or don't do the thing in the same way. If you know one way to do a thing you must know there is a better way to do the same thing.

9. If you're succeeding in anything you are doing, don't let anyone else know of your success, because if you do some other person will try to do the same thing and be your competitor.

10. When you become rich, as you will become rich if you follow my advice, don't let anyone know it. General knowledge of your wealth will only attract the taxgatherer, and other hungry people will try to get away from you something they want and something you want to keep.

11. One of the greatest assets any man can secure is a reputation for eccentricity. If you have a reputation of this kind you can do a lot of things. You can even do the things you want to do without attaching to yourself the enmity of others. Many an act which, if performed by an ordinary person, would arouse indignation, animosity and antagonism, can be performed by a man with a reputation for eccentricity with no other result than that of exciting mirth and perhaps pity. It is better to have the good will than the bad will, even of a dog.

12. Never hate anybody. Hatred is a useless expenditure of mental and nervous energy. Revenge costs much of energy and gains nothing.

13. When you find many people applauding you for what you do, and a few condemning, you can be certain that you are on the wrong course because you're doing the things that fools approve of. When the crowd ridicules and scorns you, you can at least know one thing, that it is at least possible that you are acting wisely. It is one of the instincts of men to covet applause. The wise man regulates his conduct rather by reason than by instinct.

14. It is far more important to learn what not to do than what to do. You can learn this invaluable lesson in two ways, the first of which and most inspired is by your own mistakes. The second is by observing the mistakes of others. Any man that learns all the things that he ought not to do cannot help doing the things he ought to do.

15. Posterity can never do anything for you. Therefore, you should invest nothing in posterity. Of course your heirs will quarrel over your estate, but that will be after you're dead and why should you trouble your mind over things which you will never know anything about?

16. A man can do anything he wants to do in this world, at least if he wants to do it badly enough. Therefore, I say that any of you who want to become rich can become rich if you live long enough

17. After what I have said it goes without further saying that you should save money. But no man can save himself rich. He can only make himself rich. Savings are capital. It is only by doing things that one learns how to do things. It is only the capitalist who handles capital that learns how to handle capital profitably. The more capital you have the more skillful you become as a capitalist.

18. Fools say that money makes money. I say that money does not make money. It is only men who make money.

19. There are two cardinal sins in the economic world: one is giving something for nothing, and the other is getting

> ### *Smart Habits*
> Scripps was never an effective thinker while at the office, so to stimulate the creative juices he went riding, driving, rowing, or sailing. He averaged only two to three hours per day in his newspapers' editorial rooms.

something for nothing. And the greater sin of these is getting something for nothing, or trying to do so. I really doubt if anyone ever does get something for nothing.

(Don't marry a rich wife. Women are what they are. At best they are hard enough to get along with. They are always trying to make a man do something that he doesn't want to do, and generally succeeding. When a woman is conscious of the fact that she has furnished all or any part of your capital, her influence over you will be so great as to be the worst handicap you can carry.)

20. If you're a prospective heir of your father or some other relative, you should also consider that a handicap. I would advise you to refuse to be an heir.

21. Despise not the day of small things, but rather respect the small things. It is far easier to make a profit on a very small capital invested in any business than it is to make the same proportion of profit off of a large capital. It is true that after you have learned how to make a profit on a business that shows small capital, successively, as your capital grows, you learn how to handle it profitably. Then the time will come when the greater your capital becomes in this way the greater your proportion of profits on it should be. And, for an added reason, as your wealth and skill grow rapidly, your so-called necessary expenses grow much more slowly and in time cease to grow at all, so that beyond a certain limit all your income and added income becomes a surplus, constantly to be added to your capital.

22. It is far easier to make money than to spend it. As it becomes more and more difficult to spend money, you will spend less and less of it, and hence there will be more money to accumulate.

23. The hardest labor of all labor performed by man is that of thinking. If you have become rich, train your mind to hard thinking and hold it well in leash so that your thinking will all be with but one object in view, that of accumulating more wealth.

P. T. Barnum

1810–1891

*T*he Greatest Showman on Earth was raised on a Con-
necticut farm, but decided early in life that he preferred
"laying plans for money making" over physical labor. As a
young man, he worked as a clerk for local merchants and then
bought his own shop in New York City. In 1835, he turned to
entertainment when he bought and displayed Joice Heth, a
black slave reputed to be 161 years old and to have been
George Washington's nurse. Barnum, who applied sobering
common sense to ruling over his wild empire, founded the
American Museum in New York in 1841 to display all sorts of
human curiosities and grisly items from around the world. His
coup de grace was his extravagant Barnum Circus, founded in
1871, which lives on today as The Ringling Brothers and Barnum & Bailey Circus.

Barnum's Rules for Success in Business

1. *Select the* kind *of business that suits your natural inclina-
   tions and temperament.* Some men are naturally mechan-
   ics; others have a strong aversion to anything like
   machinery, and so on; one man has a natural taste for one
   occupation, and another for another. "I am glad that we

do not all feel and think alike," said Dick Homespun, "for
if we did, everybody would think my gal, Sukey Snipes,
the sweetest creature in all creation, and they would all be
trying to court her at once."
I never could succeed as a merchant. I have tried it
unsuccessfully several times. I never could be content
with a fixed salary, for mine is a purely speculative disposition, while others are just the reverse; and therefore all
should be careful to select those occupations that suit
them best.

2. *Let your pledged word ever be sacred.* Never promise to do
a thing without performing it with the most rigid prompt-
ness. Nothing is more valuable to a man in business than
the name of always doing as he agrees, and that to the
moment. A strict adherence to this rule gives a man the
command of half the spare funds within the range of his
acquaintance, and always encircles him with a host of
friends who may be depended upon in almost any con-
ceivable emergency.

3. *Whatever you do, do with all your might.* Work at it if necessary early and late, in season and out of season, not leaving a stone unturned, and never deferring for a single hour
that which can be done just as well *now.* The old proverb
is full of truth and meaning, "Whatever is worth doing at
all, is worth doing well." Many a man acquires a fortune
by doing his business *thoroughly,* while his neighbor
remains poor for life because he only *half* does his business. Ambition, energy, industry, perseverance, are indis-
pensable requisites for success in business.

4. *Sobriety. Use no description of intoxicating drinks.* As no
man can succeed in business unless he has a *brain* to

enable him to lay his plans, and *reason* to guide him in their execution, so, no matter how bountifully a man may be blessed with intelligence, if his brain is muddled, and his judgment warped by intoxicating drinks, it is impossible for him to carry on business successfully. How many good opportunities have passed never to return, while a man was sipping a "social glass" with his friend! How many foolish bargains have been made under the influence of the *nervine* which temporarily makes its victim so *rich!* How many important chances have been put off until tomorrow, and thence for ever, because the wine-cup has thrown the system into a state of lassitude, neutralizing the energies so essential to success in business. The use of intoxicating drinks as a beverage is as much an infatuation as is the smoking of opium by the Chinese, and the former is quite as destructive to the success of the business man as the latter.

5. *Let hope predominate, but be not too visionary.* Many persons are always kept poor, because they are too *visionary.* Every project looks to them like certain success, and therefore they keep changing from one business to another, always in hot water, always "under the harrow." The plan of "counting the chickens before they are hatched" is an error of ancient date, but it does not seem to improve by age.

6. *Do not scatter your powers.* Engage in one kind of business only, and stick to it faithfully until you succeed, or until you conclude to abandon it. A constant hammering on one nail will generally drive it home at last, so that it can be clinched. When a man's undivided attention is cen-

tered on one object, his mind will constantly be suggesting improvements of value which would escape him if his
brain were occupied by a dozen different subjects at once.
Many a fortune has slipped through men's fingers by
engaging in too many occupations at once.

7. *Engage proper employees.* Never employ a man of bad
habits, when one whose habits are good can be found to
fill his situation. I have generally been extremely fortunate
in having faithful and competent persons to fill the
responsible situations in my business, and a man can
scarcely be too grateful for such a blessing. When you find
a man unfit to fill his station, either from incapacity or
peculiarity of character or disposition, dispense with his
services, and do not drag out a miserable existence in the
vain attempt to change his nature. It is utterly impossible
to do so. "You cannot make a silk purse," etc. He was created for some other sphere. Let him find and fill it.

8. *Advertise your business. Do not hide your light under a
bushel.* Whatever your occupation or calling may be, if it
needs support from the public, *advertise* it thoroughly and
efficiently, in some shape or other that will arrest public
attention. I freely confess that what success I have had in
my life may fairly be attributed more to the public press
than to nearly all other causes combined. There *may* possibly be occupations that do not require advertising, but I
cannot well conceive what they are.

Men in business will sometimes tell you that they
have tried advertising, and that it did not pay. This is only
when advertising is done sparingly and grudgingly.
Homœopathic doses of advertising will not pay perhaps—

it is like half a potion of physic, making the patient sick, but effecting nothing. Administer liberally, and the cure will be sure and permanent.

Some say they cannot afford to advertise; they mistake — they cannot afford *not* to advertise. In this country, where everybody reads the newspapers, the man must have a thick skull who does not see that these are the cheapest and best medium through which he can speak to the public, where he is to find his customers. Put on the *appearance* of business, and generally the *reality* will follow. The farmer plants his seed, and while he is sleeping, his corn and potatoes are growing. So with advertising. While you are sleeping, or eating, or conversing with one set of customers, your advertisement is being read by hundreds and thousands of persons who never saw you, nor heard of your business, and never would, had it not been for your advertisement appearing in the newspapers.

The business men of this country do not, as a general thing, appreciate the advantages of advertising thoroughly. Occasionally the public are aroused at witnessing the success of a Swaim, a Brandreth, a Townsend, a Genin, or a Root, and express astonishment at the rapidity with which these gentlemen acquire fortunes, not reflecting that the same path is open to all who *dare* pursue it. But it needs *nerve* and *faith*. The former, to enable you to launch out thousands on the uncertain waters of the future; the latter, to teach you that after many days it shall surely return, bringing an hundred or a thousand fold to him who appreciates the advantages of "printer's ink" properly applied.

9. *Avoid extravagance; and always live considerably within your income, if you can do so without absolute starvation!* It

needs no prophet to tell us that those who live fully up to their means, without any thought of a reverse in life, can never attain to a pecuniary independence.

Men and women accustomed to gratify every whim and caprice, will find it hard at first to cut down their various unnecessary expenses, and will feel it a great self-denial to live in a smaller house than they have been accustomed to, with less expensive furniture, less company, less costly clothing, a less number of balls, parties, theatre-goings, carriage ridings, pleasure excursions, cigar smokings, liquor-drinkings, etc., etc., etc.; but, after all, if they will try the plan of laying by a "nest-egg," or in other words, a small sum of money, after paying all expenses, they will be surprised at the plea-

Outrageous Promotion

Barnum once asked an acquaintance to sue him for fraud for displaying a *supposed* bearded lady. When the case hit the courts it was a hit: The bearded lady proved to be legitimate, the newspapers had a field day, and the public thronged to Barnum's museum to see her.

sure to be derived from constantly adding to their little "pile," as well as from all the economical habits which follow in the pursuit of this peculiar pleasure.

The old suit of clothes, and the old bonnet and dress, will answer for another season; the Croton or spring water will taste better than champagne; a brisk walk will prove more exhilarating than a ride in the finest coach; a social family chat, an evening's reading in the family circle, or an hour's play of "hunt the slipper" and "blind man's buff," will be far more pleasant than a fifty- or a five-hundred-dollar party, when the reflection on the *difference in cost* is indulged in by those who begin to know the *pleasures of saving*.

Thousands of men are kept poor, and tens of thousands are made so after they have acquired quite sufficient to support them well through life, in consequence of laying their plans of living on too expensive a platform. Some families in this country expend twenty thousand dollars per annum, and some much more, and would scarcely know how to live on a less sum.

Prosperity is a more severe ordeal than adversity, especially sudden prosperity. "Easy come, easy go" is an old and true proverb. *Pride*, when permitted full sway, is the great undying cankerworm which gnaws the very vitals of a man's worldly possessions, let them be small or great, hundreds or millions. Many persons, as they begin to prosper, immediately commence expending for luxuries, until in a short time their expenses swallow up their income, and they become ruined in their ridiculous attempts to keep up appearances, and make a "sensation."

I know a gentleman of fortune, who says, that when he first began to prosper, his wife *would have* a new and elegant sofa. "That sofa," he says, "cost me thirty thousand dollars!" The riddle is thus explained:

When the sofa reached the house, it was found necessary to get chairs to "match," then sideboards, carpets, and tables, "to correspond" with them, and so on through the entire stock of furniture, when at last it was found that the house itself was quite too small and old-fashioned for the furniture, and a new one was built to correspond with the sofa and *et ceteras*; "thus," added my friend, "running up an outlay of thirty thousand dollars caused by that single sofa, and saddling on me, in the shape of servants, equipage, and the necessary expenses attendant upon keeping up a fine 'establishment,' a yearly outlay of eleven thousand dollars, and a tight pinch at that; whereas, ten years ago, we lived with much more real comfort, because much less care, on as many hundreds. The truth is," he continued, "that sofa would have brought me to inevitable bankruptcy, had not a most unexampled tide of prosperity kept me above it."

10. *Do not depend upon others.* Your success must depend upon your own individual exertions. Trust not to the assistance of friends; but learn that every man must be the architect of his own fortune.

    With proper attention to the foregoing rules, and such observations as a man of sense will pick up in his own experience, the road to competence will not, I think, usually be found a difficult one.

Sam Walton

1918–1992

*T*he founder of Wal-Mart grew up in a poor farm community of rural Missouri, right in the heart of the dust bowl of the Great Depression. After attending the University of Missouri, Sam Walton joined JCPenney. World War II service interrupted his career, after which he bought his own variety store, called Ben Franklin, with $5,000 of his own money and $20,000 that he borrowed from his father-in-law. Five years later, he sold it and opened Walton's 5 & 10 in Bentonville, Arkansas. He opened a second five-and-ten in 1952 and introduced the concept of self-service into retail to keep costs down. Not until 1962 did Walton open his first Wal-Mart. The company went public in 1970, and in 1985, Forbes magazine named Walton the richest man in America. A great motivator, he never ceased playing cheerleader in building his business.

Sam's Rules for Building a Business

Rule 1: Commit to your business. Believe in it more than anybody else. I think I overcame every single one of my personal shortcomings by the sheer passion I brought to my work. I don't know if you're born with this kind of passion, or if you can learn it. But I do know you need it. If you love your work, you'll be out there every day trying to do it the best you possibly can, and pretty soon everybody around will catch the passion from you—like a fever.

Rule 2: Share your profits with all your associates, and treat them as partners. In turn, they will treat you as a partner, and together you will all perform beyond your wildest expectations. Remain a corporation and retain control if you like, but behave as a servant leader in a partnership. Encourage your associates to hold a stake in the company. Offer discounted stock, and grant them stock for their retirement. It's the single best thing we ever did.

Rule 3: Motivate your partners. Money and ownership alone aren't enough. Constantly, day by day, think of new and more interesting ways to motivate and challenge your partners. Set high goals, encourage competition, and then keep score. Make bets with outrageous payoffs. If things get stale, cross-pollinate; have managers switch jobs with one another to stay challenged. Keep everybody guessing as to what your next trick is going to be. Don't become too predictable.

> ### *Outrageous Promotion*
> Walton, who once dressed in a hula skirt to do a hula dance on Wall Street, encouraged a carnival-like atmosphere at his stores. For example, one store played hide-and-seek with a TV set. If you could find the TV (hidden somewhere in the store) you could buy it for 22 cents. The result: 500 to 600 customers stampeded the store and a pile of merchandise was sold.

Rule 4: Communicate everything you possibly can to your partners. The more they know, the more they'll understand. The more they understand, the more they'll care. Once they care, there's no stopping them. If you don't trust your associates to know what's going on, they'll know you don't really consider them partners. Information is power, and the gain you get from empowering your associates more than offsets the risk of informing your competitors.

Rule 5: Appreciate everything your associates do for the business. A paycheck and a stock option will buy one kind of loyalty. But all of us like to be told how much somebody appreciates what we do for them. We like to hear it often, and especially when we have done something we're really proud of. Nothing else can quite substitute for a few well-chosen, well-timed, sincere words of praise. They're absolutely free—and worth a fortune.

Rule 6: Celebrate your successes. Find some humor in your failures. Don't take yourself so seriously. Loosen up, and everybody around you will loosen up. Have fun. Show enthusiasm—always. When all else fails, put on a costume and sing a silly song. Then make everybody else sing with you. Don't do a hula on Wall Street. It's been done. Think up your own stunt. All of this is more important, and more fun, than you think, and it really fools the competition. "Why should we take those cornballs at Wal-Mart seriously?"

Rule 7: Listen to everyone in your company. And figure out ways to get them talking. The folks on the front lines—the ones who actually talk to the customer—are the only ones who really know what's going on out there. You'd better find out what they know. This really is what total quality is all about. To push responsibility down in your organization, and to force good ideas to bubble up within it, you *must* listen to what your associates are trying to tell you.

Rule 8: Exceed your customers' expectations. If you do, they'll come back over and over. Give them what they want—and a little more. Let them know you appreciate them. Make good on all your mistakes, and don't make excuses—apologize. Stand behind everything you do. The two most important words I ever wrote were on that first Wal-Mart sign: "Satisfaction Guaranteed." They're still up there, and they have made all the difference.

Rule 9: Control your expenses better than your competition. This is where you can always find the competitive advantage. For twenty-five years running—long before Wal-Mart was known as the nation's largest retailer—we ranked number one in our industry for the lowest ratio of expenses to sales. You can make a lot of different mistakes and still recover if you run an efficient operation. Or you can be brilliant and still go out of business if you're too inefficient.

Rule 10: Swim upstream. Go the other way. Ignore the conventional wisdom. If everybody else is doing it one way, there's a good chance you can find your niche by going in exactly the opposite direction. But be prepared for a lot of folks to wave you down and tell you you're headed the wrong way. I guess in all my years, what I heard more often than anything was: a town of less than 50,000 population cannot support a discount store for very long.

Henry Ford
1863–1947

*H*enry Ford grew up on a farm, but was always fascinated by mechanical things. As a boy, he built his own watch and operated a steam-powered thrasher for a neighboring farmer whose workers feared it. His father gave him land, hoping he'd too be a farmer, but Ford left for Detroit to work for the Edison Company, where he rose to a superintendency position. In 1899, he left Thomas Edison's company to experiment full-time with motor cars. Not until the age of 40 did he found his own company—twice before investors had pulled out. Ford, who devoutly believed in providing the customer quality and service, introduced the durable and best-selling Model T in 1908. Five years later, he instituted the conveyor belt assembly line in his factory, which cut production time per car down from 12-plus hours to 1½ hours.

Principles of Service

1. An absence of fear of the future and of veneration for the past. One who fears the future, who fears failure, limits his activities. Failure is only the opportunity more intelligently to begin again. There is no disgrace in honest fail-

ure; there is disgrace in fearing to fail. What is past is useful only as it suggests ways and means for progress.

2. A disregard of competition. Whoever does a thing best ought to be the one to do it. It is criminal to try to get business away from another man — criminal because one is then trying to lower for personal gain the condition of one's fellow man — to rule by force instead of by intelligence.

3. The putting of service before profit. Without a profit, business cannot extend. There is nothing inherently wrong about making a profit. Well-conducted business enterprise cannot fail to return a profit, but profit must and inevitably will come as a reward for good service. It cannot be the basis — it must be the result of service.

> ### Outrageous Promotion
>
> To prove his car design was the best and to attract both investors and customers, Ford took to what was then the extremely dangerous sport of auto racing. A week before New York's grand auto show, he even broke the current time record for one mile when he ran his "Model B" full throttle across a frozen lake.

4. Manufacturing is not buying low and selling high. It is the process of buying materials fairly and, with the smallest possible addition of cost, transforming those materials into a consumable product and giving it to the consumer. Gambling, speculating, and sharp dealing, tend only to clog this progression.

Robert Mondavi

1913–

*The founder of the Robert Mondavi Winery in Napa Valley
is one of the most respected leaders in the industry. Mondavi's parents immigrated to the United States from Italy, and
in 1919, the family moved to California, where his father went
into the grape business, buying and shipping the fruit east.
Mondavi, whose philosophy for success includes foremost having faith in yourself, studied economics and business administration at Stanford University. After graduating, he immersed
himself in the winery business, but not until 1943 did he, his
brother, and his father buy their own vineyard, the Charles
Krug winery. A family feud resulted in Mondavi leaving the
family winery in 1965. At age 52, he struck out on his own,
determined to compete with the best European wines.*

Basic Components for Success

People often ask me, "Bob, what are the secrets to your success? What are the biggest lessons you have to share with people who are starting out or trying to remake their lives?" Well,
as I've tried to illustrate in the preceding chapters, in my philosophy of life there are some basic tenets that I believe lead to
success in business—and in almost every other life endeavor.

To succeed in business or in life I don't think you need fancy schooling or highly technical expertise. What you need is common sense, a commitment to hard work, and the courage to go your own way. This is the necessary foundation. On top of this foundation, there are fifteen other qualities that have served me well, and I think of them now as the basic components of my philosophy for success:

- First and foremost, you must have confidence and faith in yourself.
- Second, whatever you choose to do, make a commitment to excel, and then pour yourself into it with your heart and soul and complete dedication.
- Third, interest is not enough—you must be passionate about what you do if you want to succeed and have a happy life. Find a job you love and you'll never have to work a day in your life.
- Fourth, establish a goal just beyond what you think you can do. When you achieve that, establish another and another. This will teach you to embrace risk.

Extreme Measures

To iron out their differences in managing the family winery, Mondavi and his two sons went to see a psychotherapist. The result: Mondavi became more of a father and mentor, not a micromanager.

- Fifth, be completely honest and open. I never had secrets. I would share my knowledge and experience with others if they would share with me. I always had confidence that there was enough room for all of us.
- Sixth, generosity pays. So learn to initiate giving. What you give will enrich your life and come back to you many times over.

- Seventh, only make promises and commitments you know you can keep. A broken promise can damage your credibility and reputation beyond repair.
- Eighth, you must understand that you cannot change people. You might be able to influence them a little, but you can't change anyone but yourself. So accept people the way they are. Accept their differences and try to work with them as they are. I learned this late in life, and it is amazing what peace of mind I found when I finally understood it.
- Ninth, to live and work in harmony with others, don't be judgmental. Instead, cultivate tolerance, empathy, and compassion. And never berate people, especially your children, in front of their cohorts. This can be dispiriting and damaging to them, and it's counterproductive for you. As I've learned, if you want to teach someone to fly, you don't start by clipping his wings.
- Tenth, human beings experience the same thing in very different ways. Two people can live through the exact same experience and come away with totally different understandings of what happened. So between people there is always a large space for misunderstanding. Always be alert for misunderstandings and tread lightly, especially when it comes to politics, religion, or moral standards.
- Eleventh, it is very important that we understand one another. We need to learn how to bridge those spaces of misunderstanding. To do this, listen carefully, and when you talk, be sure people understand you. On important issues, have people repeat back to you what you've said, to make sure there are no areas of confusion or conflict.
- Twelfth, rarely will you find complete harmony between two human beings. But if you find it, maintaining this harmony

requires individuals or soul mates to have complete confidence in one another. Make time to be alone, to share experiences and appreciate together precious moments and the beauty of life. Open all of yourself to that person — emotionally, physically, spiritually, and intellectually. And always, always leave time for playfulness and laughter. There is no better tonic for keeping love alive and vibrant than laughter and good cheer.

- Thirteenth, in both life and work, stay flexible. Whether in a country, a company, or a family, the same holds true: Dictatorship and rigidity rarely work. Freedom and elasticity do.
- Fourteenth, always stay positive. Use your common sense. And remember this: America was built on the can-do spirit and will continue to thrive on the can-do spirit.
- Fifteenth, out of all the rigidities and mistakes of my past, I've learned one final lesson, and I'd like to see it engraved on the desk of every business leader, teacher, and parent in America:

The greatest leaders don't rule. They inspire.

Victor Kiam

1926–

*V*ictor Kiam made a name for himself by appearing in his own TV ads and declaring that he loved the Remington razor so much, he bought the company in 1978. After he graduated from Harvard Business School in 1951, he joined Lever Brothers as a management trainee. For four years, he found himself selling cosmetics to backcountry pharmacists, who had a habit of mixing up cold medicines in their basement that "had the kick of low-grade bourbon." Kiam jumped companies to Playtex in 1955 and rose to the position of executive vice president. But then, in 1968, he attended a conference that included a panel discussion on entrepreneurship. Kiam was so enthralled with the speakers that he quit Playtex that same year to pursue his own interests, but not before looking at himself in the mirror and asking some hard questions.

The Man-in-the-Mirror Test

What does it take to be an entrepreneur? Do you have the go-getter's version of the right stuff? To find out, all you have to do is take the advice found in a Michael Jackson hit song. Consult your "Man in the Mirror" and ask:

1. Do I Have Confidence in Myself: You have to believe you can move the Himalayas if that is what your ultimate success demands. In a corporation, you'll want the people working for or with you to follow your lead. You want your superiors to give you as much authority as you can handle. They have to respect your judgment.

   If you're running your own enterprise, you may want investors. Your clients have to believe you will do your very best work for them or that your products are of the highest quality. They have to catch your enthusiasm. How can you pump them up if you don't believe in yourself? As an entrepreneur, you always want to stand out. How can you hold center stage if you don't think yourself worthy of it?

2. Do I Have Confidence in My Venture: When you make an investment in an enterprise, what are you betting on? The idea or the people behind it? The answer is always both. Your time is one of your most valuable commodities. If you become involved in a venture it must be worth your total commitment. If you start a venture plagued by doubts, you are going to run into the self-fulfilling prophecy. When the hard times hit—and, believe me, even the most successful entrepreneur encounters some turbulence on his flight to paradise—you are going to be hard pressed to give your project the support it needs if you doubt its chances for survival.

3. Are You Willing to Make Sacrifices: Nine to five has no real meaning for you. An entrepreneur is not a clock watcher. Business is a game. You will often need more than eight hours to score the winning touchdown.

4. Am I a Decision Maker: You have to be. An entrepreneur wants to assume the ultimate responsibility for his or her project. The buck not only stops at the true entrepreneur's desk, it starts there also. You are often on your own. If you're running a business or a division, no one can make the tough decisions for you.

5. Do I Recognize Opportunity: This is vital. Are you often berating yourself because you've passed by yet another chance of a lifetime? You can't allow too many of those to slip by. Get used to looking over all the nuances of every proposition. Approach each idea thinking, "How can I make this work for me?"

6. Can I Keep My Cool: Do you feel a bit of tightness in your throat when pressure is applied to you? Do the butterflies flap up a Wagnerian opera whenever crunch time comes? That's OK, it's a typically human response. But do others around you pick up on that nervousness? If they do, you could be in trouble. The entrepreneur is a general. If his troops are about to enter the valley of death, his mere presence must say, "Our strategy is sound. This army is ready. We will fight our way through this dangerous terrain without serious casualties." Your army will be able to take a cool, reasoned approach to any obstacle. Such a stance represents the first step toward winning. On the other hand, if your troops sense you are as bewildered as they are, that the hand mapping the strategy is an unsteady one, you are in big trouble. While you might delude yourself that you are still a leader of men, you will rapidly discover there are no men left to lead.

7. Do I Have High Levels of Energy and Stamina: Entrepreneurs shouldn't have any shortage of energy. We're much

too involved; we feed off life's opportunities. If you find yourself looking forward to your afternoon siesta or constantly thinking about the nice warm tub waiting for you at the end of the day, don't even think about getting into the entrepreneurial life. While you're napping or unwinding in the bath, some competitor is out on the prowl and picking up points at your expense. Remember, you can't always

---

Outrageous Promotion

To ensure that his would-be customers remembered his pitch, Kiam rented a monkey to bring along on sales calls.

---

outthink, outplan, or outspend a rival. But you can outwork anyone.

8. Am I Willing to Lead by Example: You can't ask your troops to walk on water for you if you choose to ride the *Queen Mary* over the same route. You want your team to put in fourteen-hour workdays when it is needed? Make sure you are willing to do the same. I've never asked an employee to do something I wasn't willing to do. I feel a responsibility to work harder than the people who work for me.

While we're on the subject, never, ever ask an employee to act as a gofer. When I am on the road with one of my salesmen and he tries to take my bag, he has a real fight on his hands. I just won't give it to him. I want him to know we are partners and that we are in this thing together. You want to motivate the people around you. Leading by example is one of the best methods.

Lillian Vernon
1927–

Very few mailboxes have not received Lillian Vernon catalogs, which are renowned for striking the consumers' tastes. However, Vernon's tale is one of both triumph and tragedy. She was born in Germany, where her father had built a prosperous lingerie business, but when Hitler came to power in 1933, life changed dramatically for this Jewish family. After her older brother was attacked by Nazi thugs, they emigrated to Amsterdam and then to the United States. Vernon's brother was later killed in World War II, but she persevered through the tragedy. Married and pregnant in 1951, Vernon was convinced that she had some greater purpose in the working world and decided to start her mail-order business with $2,000. With the odds stacked against her as a woman entrepreneur in the 1950s, Vernon's catchwords became commitment and hard work.

Are You an Entrepreneur?

If you're thinking of starting your own business, here are ten questions you should ask yourself before you begin. Your answers should help you make your decision.

1. Do you have the necessary commitment? To succeed, you must feel passionate about the work you have chosen.

Lukewarm enthusiasm will not sustain you through the challenges you will face in a start-up business.

2. Are you prepared to work extremely hard? Launching your own business demands long hours of labor. Are you sure you want to give up a good part of your social life: your weekends, golf games, and vacations? For your developing business to succeed, you will need to focus all your energies on it.

3. Are you sure you have the mental stamina and concentration to meet the demands your project will impose on you? If your attention flags, you may jeopardize your venture.

> ### Outrageous Promotion
> Lillian Vernon created the waspy-sounding name of her company by combining her first name with Mount Vernon, the name of the Westchester County, New York, town where she lived as a newly-wed. She later legally changed her own name from Lillian Hochberg to the company's name.

4. Do you accept new ideas easily? Do you treat other people's ideas with respect? Are you able to make decisions right away? An entrepreneur must be open-minded, flexible, and able to respond to new ideas.

5. How do you deal with problem solving? Are you prepared to spend time analyzing a problem and finding a solution? Or do you just close your eyes and hope for the best? No matter how carefully you plan, you are bound to run into an unforeseen problem now and then. Be prepared to cope with such a situation.

6. Are you ready to commit to the long term? A company's success is never an overnight miracle. That is one reason you must be absolutely certain that you love your work—there will be a lot of it.

7. What back-up resources do you have? Banks and other financial institutions seldom lend money to start-up businesses. Will family members or friends invest in your company or tide you over during a rough patch?

8. Are you good at concentrating on detail? Often, no one but you will be able to take care of small items. An entrepreneur's life is not one of ideas alone.

9. Are you ready to sit down and write a careful analysis of your business prospects? Without a best case/worst case scenario to guide you through the first years, you may be in for an unpleasant surprise or two. Be aware and be prepared.

10. Are you by nature an optimist? Mistakes and setbacks are bound to occur. Can you—without getting derailed or discouraged—learn from your mistakes?

PART VI

~

The Gurus

Warren Bennis

1925–

A s founding chairman of The Leadership Institute at the University of Southern California's Marshall School of Business, where he has taught since 1979, Warren Bennis is recognized the world over as an expert on leadership. Bennis, who has written more than 25 books and 1,500 articles on management and leadership, earned his undergraduate degree from Antioch College in 1951 and a Ph.D. from MIT in 1955. He stayed at MIT for several years as a faculty member of the Sloan School of Management and then taught at Harvard and Boston Universities. Bennis himself took a management job as president of the University of Cincinnati, before heading west.

Five Key Skills

1. The ability to accept people as they are, not as you would like them to be. In a way, this can be seen as the height of wisdom—to "enter the skin" of someone else, to understand what other people are like on *their* terms, rather than judging them.

2. The capacity to approach relationships and problems in terms of the present rather than the past. Certainly it is true that we can learn from past mistakes. But using the

present as a takeoff point for trying to make fewer mistakes seemed to be more productive for our leaders—and certainly was more psychologically sound than rehashing things that are over.

3. The ability to treat those who are close to you with the same courteous attention that you extend to strangers and casual acquaintances. The need for this skill is often most obvious—and lacking—in our relationships with our own families. But it is equally important at work. We tend to take for granted those to whom we are closest. Often we get so accustomed to seeing them and hearing from them that we lose our ability to listen to what they are really saying or to appreciate the quality—good or bad—of what they are doing. Personal feelings of friendship or hostility or simple indifference interfere.

    There are two aspects to this problem of overfamiliarity. The first is that of not hearing what is being said: selective deafness leads to misunderstandings, misconceptions, mistakes. The second is the matter of feedback we fail to provide to indicate our attentiveness.

4. The ability to trust others, even if the risk seems great. A withholding of trust is often necessary for self-protection. But the price is too high if it means always being on guard, constantly suspicious of others. Even an overdose of trust that at times involves the risk of being deceived or disappointed is wiser, in the long run, than taking it for granted that most people are incompetent or insincere.

5. The ability to do without constant approval and recognition from others. Particularly in a work situation, the need for constant approval can be harmful and counterproductive. It should not really matter how many people *like* leaders. The

important thing is the quality of work that results from collaborating with them. The emotionally wise leader realizes that this quality will suffer when undue emphasis is placed on being a "good guy." More important, it is a large part of the leader's job to take risks. And risks by their very nature cannot be pleasing to everyone.

Smart Habits

To force yourself to reflect on and learn from your experiences, especially failures, Bennis recommends keeping a diary and reading biographies—biographies, he believes, inspire self-reflection.

Dale Carnegie
1888–1955

*D*ale Carnegie is best remembered for his ever-popular public speaking courses and his 1937 book, How to Win Friends and Influence People, *which sold over 1.3 million copies alone before his death. He was raised on a Missouri farm and joined the high school debate team. However, after attending the State Teachers' College in Missouri, Carnegie pursued a career in sales. As a salesman for the International Correspondence School, he sold only one course before quitting, and then moved to Chicago to work in sales at Armour & Co. From there, it was to New York City in 1911, where he tried his hand at acting. Finally, Carnegie started teaching public speaking at a YMCA, during which time he refined his ideas on how to lead people without commanding them. He then founded the Carnegie Institute for Effective Speaking and Human Relations.*

Be a Leader

A leader's job often includes changing your people's attitudes and behavior. Some suggestions to accomplish this:

PRINCIPLE 1
Begin with praise and honest appreciation.

PRINCIPLE 2
Call attention to people's mistakes indirectly.

PRINCIPLE 3
Talk about your own mistakes before criticizing the other person.

PRINCIPLE 4
Ask questions instead of giving direct orders.

> *Outrageous Promotion*
> Not long before delivering a lecture at Carnegie Hall, Dale changed the spelling of his name from *Carnegey* to *Carnegie* so that his audience would associate him with the highly successful king of steel, Andrew Carnegie.

PRINCIPLE 5
Let the other person save face.

PRINCIPLE 6
Praise the slightest improvement and praise every improvement. Be "hearty in your approbation and lavish in your praise."

PRINCIPLE 7
Give the other person a fine reputation to live up to.

PRINCIPLE 8
Use encouragement. Make the fault seem easy to correct.

PRINCIPLE 9
Make the other person happy about doing the thing you suggest.

Peter F. Drucker

1909–

*P*eter Drucker, management-consultant extraordinaire, was born in Vienna where his father was a prominent lawyer. Drucker studied law at the University of Hamburg and at the University of Frankfurt in Germany. When Adolf Hitler came to power in 1933, he knew it was time to leave Germany. For the next four years he worked in England as an economist, and then in 1937, his wife and he emigrated to the United States. At the outbreak of World War II, a series of insightful articles on Germany's economy written by Drucker caught the attention of both Washington's policy makers and U.S. business leaders, enabling him to launch his consulting business in 1940. Drucker also taught at Bennington College, New York University, and the Claremont Graduate School in California.

Lessons for Leading People

The three people from whom I learned the most in my work were all very different. The first two were exceptionally demanding; the third was exceptionally brilliant. All three taught me a lot.

My first boss founded the economics department in a European private bank. He went to France when Hitler came to power, rose to be a full general under De Gaulle, and commanded French resistance troops in Africa. The second was among the last in the great 19th-century tradition of liberal journalism in Europe, a stern disciplinarian. I learned more from him than from anybody else. The third was a London banker who built a private bank from scratch. It became the first newcomer to the London Clearinghouse Association—the club of private banks—in 50 years, and today is part of a financial conglomerate. Five lessons from those remarkable men still apply today:

- *Treat people differently, based on their strengths.* My first boss, the banker, simply didn't know that there were such things as beginners, and so he had me work out a merger of the European artificial silk industry—rayon, the first synthetic. It was a merger of the German and Dutch, Italian and French companies. And at age 19 I worked it out, period. I was a securities analyst trainee and knew nothing about anything. When I went in to ask a question he looked at me and said, "Have you looked it up? Don't come and ask me a question until after you have looked it up." So I looked things up, and I learned something.

    There were four or five of us, and he treated each of us differently—the way we needed to be treated, which for me was very rough. He demanded enormous things from me. He looked at people, what they should be doing, and then demanded it at a high professional level, far beyond our capacity, and did not stop until we did work that had that quality.
- *Set high standards, but give people the freedom and responsibility to do their jobs.* My next job was for Frankfurt's leading afternoon newspaper. It was the second largest afternoon paper on the continent—a 600,000 circulation, with an editorial staff of

14 people. We didn't know enough to know that we were over-worked; we just loved it.

I went to work as financial and foreign writer on my 20th birthday. The oldest was perhaps 26—largely because this was 10 years after the end of World War I, and the people that should have held those jobs were lying in officers' graves all over Europe. There were no educated 30-year-olds, literally none.

You began work at 6:00 in the morning. I took the first streetcar, which stopped outside the office at 6:02. My first morning I climbed up the three stairs to the editorial offices and there was the editor, 6 foot 5, whom I had never met—the publisher had hired me—with a watch in his hand looking at me. He said, "Young man, if you don't come in five minutes to six tomorrow morning you don't have to come in at all." I explained that the first streetcar didn't leave until 5:35. He picked up the telephone at 6:00 in the morning and got the mayor of Frankfurt out of bed. The next day the first streetcar left at 5:07, and I was on it.

I had a 6:50 deadline each morning—less than an hour in which to write the second and third editorials each day, six days a week. One needed to be 900 words, the other 600 words. The editor had to approve them, but the topics were entirely up to me—and did I learn. The discipline this imposed forced me to be resourceful, but allowed me to be creative. Yes, the editor was stern, forbidding, demanding, relentless. But his demands were based not on the mindless exercise of authority but on accountability and the delivery of results.

- *Performance review must be honest, exacting, and an integral part of the job.* The same editor provided a very powerful performance-assessment model. The fourth Saturday of every month, instead of going home at noon, when the paper had gone to press, we adjourned to a private room in a tavern and stayed until 2:00 in the morning. We paid for the sausages they served; the beer was furnished by the paper.

So we began around the table. The first was usually the one woman on the staff, because her name began with a B. We each made a presentation about the last month's work, what we thought we had done outstandingly well and why, what we thought needed improvement, where we had botched things, and what we could learn from those.

It was not just a performance review, it was a performance, period. Each of us—all 14—took 20 or 30 minutes. That's seven hours. The editor didn't say a word; we all asked questions, and he only took a few notes. So by that time, we had another round of sausage and beer. Then the editor would ask for comments, 10 minutes or 15 minutes from each of us. Finally he would sum up for three hours without once looking at the notes. We just loved it—and learned everything there was to know about where we stood and how to do better.

- *People learn the most when teaching others.* My third employer was the youngest of three senior partners of a bank. I mostly worked for him as the firm's economist and London securities analyst.

Once a week or so, he would sit down with me and talk about the way he saw the world. He used me as an audience, and in the process, he demonstrated how to think. He talked the same subject over and over again until it clicked. I learned an enormous amount listening to him and seeing a first-rate mind work. The clarity, the aesthetic rigor he demanded of himself was a joy to behold.

He insisted that since I was the firm's economist, I had better learn some economics, which as a brash young man I thought was quite unreasonable. But he used his influence to get me into a prestigious economics seminar at Cambridge. When I left the firm I told him, "I'm not going to be a banker; money bores me silly." He said, "I've known that all along." He simply needed someone who could listen, who could allow him to work out his ideas. In the end, I think he learned more than I did from our little talks.

> ### Savvy Leadership
> To measure employees' development, Drucker espouses designing a scorecard. It should judge expectations against actual performance, especially for those employees who are promoted.

- *Effective leaders earn respect—but they don't need to be liked.* Each of my three mentors won my respect, but I doubt any of them considered himself my friend. It would never have occurred to the editor, for instance, to feel affection for a staff member; it was irrelevant. At the end he made me one of three senior editors, but I never even had lunch with him. I never sat down with him except on business. Yet I knew that if I did my job I could trust him totally—and that if I didn't, I would be out, period.

When I went back to Europe in 1953 for the first time since the war, I went to Frankfurt and called on him. He was very gracious, and I told him how much he taught me in those monthly review sessions, how much I learned. And he looked at me and said, "That never occurred to me. The only thing I was interested in was next month's papers." The only bond we had was the task at hand.

★

Each of these three leaders taught me valuable lessons. But they were, to use an often-abused phrase, "just doing their jobs." They focused on performance and responsibility for results. Intuitively, they understood that the manager's job is to make human strength effective and human weakness irrelevant. Perhaps that was the biggest lesson of all.

Tom Peters

1942–

*T**om Peters coauthored* In Search of Excellence, *an instant best-seller in 1982 that went on to become the most successful management book of all time, spending three years on the* New York Times *best-seller list. After attending Cornell University, where he played lacrosse and earned a bachelor's degree in 1965 and a master's degree in industrial engineering in 1966, Peters joined the war in Vietnam as a member of the U.S. Navy's construction battalion. He then continued his education, earning an MBA and a Ph.D. from Stanford University. Between degrees, Peters joined the venerable consulting firm of McKinsey & Co. in 1974. Although* In Search of Excellence *was based on his consulting work, Peters left McKinsey the year before the book was published to found his own consulting firm, the Tom Peters Group.*

Eight Attributes of Innovative Companies

1. *A bias for action,* for getting on with it. Even though these companies may be analytical in their approach to decision making, they are not paralyzed by that fact (as so many others seem to be). In many of these companies the standard operating procedure is "Do it, fix it, try it." Says a Digital

Equipment Corporation senior executive, for example, "When we've got a big problem here, we grab ten senior guys and stick them in a room for a week. They come up with an answer *and* implement it." Moreover, the companies are experimenters supreme. Instead of allowing 250 engineers and marketers to work on a new product in isolation for fifteen months, they form bands of 5 to 25 and test ideas out on a customer, often with inexpensive prototypes, within a matter of weeks. What is striking is the host of practical devices the excellent companies employ, to maintain corporate fleetness of foot and counter the stultification that almost inevitably comes with size.

2. *Close to the customer.* These companies learn from the people they serve. They provide unparalleled quality, service, and reliability—things that work and last. They succeed in differentiating—*à la* Frito-Lay (potato chips), Maytag (washers), or Tupperware—the most commodity-like products. IBM's marketing vice president, Francis G. (Buck) Rodgers, says, "It's a shame that, in so many companies, whenever you get good service, it's an exception." Not so at the excellent companies. Everyone gets into the act. Many of the innovative companies got their best product ideas from customers. That comes from listening, intently and regularly.

3. *Autonomy and entrepreneurship.* The innovative companies foster many leaders and many innovators throughout the organization. They are a hive of what we've come to call champions; 3M has been described as "so intent on innovation that its essential atmosphere seems not like that of a large corporation but rather a loose network of laboratories and cubbyholes populated by feverish inventors and

dauntless entrepreneurs who let their imaginations fly in all directions." They don't try to hold everyone on so short a rein that he can't be creative. They encourage practical risk taking, and support good tries. They follow Fletcher Byrom's ninth commandment: "Make sure you generate a reasonable number of mistakes."

Extreme Measures

To cultivate "out-of-the-box thinking," Peters advises taking vacations to the Far East or other exotic places (as opposed to two weeks at the beach), trying unique food, listening to foreign languages, noticing how the people act, and generally exploring things that are strange to you.

---

4. *Productivity through people.* The excellent companies treat the rank and file as the root source of quality and productivity gain. They do not foster we/they labor attitudes or regard capital investment as the fundamental source of efficiency improvement. As Thomas J. Watson, Jr., said of his company, "IBM's philosophy is largely contained in three simple beliefs. I want to begin with what I think is the most important: *our respect for the individual.* This is a simple concept, but in IBM it occupies a major portion of management time." Texas Instruments' chairman Mark Shepherd talks about it in terms of every worker being "seen as a source of ideas, not just acting as a pair of hands"; each of his more than 9,000 People Involvement Program, or PIP, teams (TI's quality circles) does contribute to the company's sparkling productivity record.

5. *Hands-on, value driven.* Thomas Watson, Jr., said that "the basic philosophy of an organization has far more to do with its achievements than do technological or economic resources, organizational structure, innovation and timing." Watson

and HP's William Hewlett are legendary for walking the plant floors. McDonald's Ray Kroc regularly visits stores and assesses them on the factors the company holds dear, Q.S.C. & V. (Quality, Service, Cleanliness, and Value).

6. *Stick to the knitting.* Robert W. Johnson, former Johnson & Johnson chairman, put it this way: "Never acquire a business you don't know how to run." Or as Edward G. Harness, past chief executive at Procter & Gamble, said, "This company has never left its base. We seek to be anything but a conglomerate." While there were a few exceptions, the odds for excellent performance seem strongly to favor those companies that stay reasonably close to businesses they know.

7. *Simple form, lean staff.* As big as most of the companies we have looked at are, none when we looked at it was formally run with a matrix organization structure, and some which had tried that form had abandoned it. The underlying structural forms and systems in the excellent companies are elegantly simple. Top-level staffs are lean; it is not uncommon to find a corporate staff of fewer than 100 people running multi-billion-dollar enterprises.

8. *Simultaneous loose-tight properties.* The excellent companies are both centralized and decentralized. For the most part, as we have said, they have pushed autonomy down to the shop floor or product development team. On the other hand, they are fanatic centralists around the few core values they hold dear. 3M is marked by barely organized chaos surrounding its product champions. Yet one analyst argues, "The brainwashed members of an extremist religious sect are no more conformist in their central beliefs." At Digital the chaos is so rampant that one executive

noted, "Damn few people know who they work for." Yet Digital's fetish for reliability is more rigidly adhered to than any outsider could imagine.

Most of these eight attributes are not startling. Some, if not most, are "motherhoods." But as Rene McPherson says, "Almost everybody agrees, 'people are our most important asset.' Yet almost none really lives it."

Savvy Leadership

At his consulting company, no one is allowed a business card with their title on it. Peters' point: all are significant contributors.

Joseph Juran
1904–

*N*o other management expert has influenced the drive for quality like Joseph Juran, a consultant since 1945 and founder of The Juran Institute. He was born in Romania. His father, however, left for the United States in 1909, and it took him three years to save enough money to bring the whole family over. Juran excelled at math and, at age 11, he was a bookkeeper for an icehouse to help support the family. Fortunately, his father became a bootlegger in 1919, which helped fund Juran's education at the University of Minnesota. After graduating, he took a quality control job with Western Electric in Chicago. At the end of World War II, he realized that he could go no further within a corporate structure, so Juran struck out on his own. Over the years, in consulting for others, he's discovered that successful executives share common traits.

Thirteen Common Success Factors

- They make product quality and customer service their priorities. Quality becomes top priority among company goals, and customer satisfaction becomes the focus in customer relations.
- They train all managers in quality improvement processes. This training usually starts at the top and then cascades down.

- They enlarge the business plan to include quality-related goals—goals to improve customer satisfaction, to meet competitive standards, to reduce costs of poor quality, and to improve key processes.
- They use benchmarking as a means of setting ambitious (but attainable) goals.
- They identify the actions needed to meet the goals. They also assign clear responsibility for taking those actions, and they provide the needed resources.
- They accelerate the pace of quality improvement far beyond prior practice. This translates to thousands of improvements annually—a revolutionary pace. Every improvement project includes business processes as well as factory processes.
- They develop new measures for quality. For example, in its early years, Xerox was stunningly successful financially. Its executives were well supplied with financial measures— sales, profits, return on investment, and the like. However, they lacked such essential measures of quality as customer satisfaction and competitive quality. Lacking such measures, they learned of their quality problems only after severe damage had already been done, making their comeback all the more remarkable.
- They regularly review performance against quality goals, just as they review performance against financial goals.
- They publicly acknowledge persons and teams who achieve superior performance.
- Self-audits. They use self-audits to identify the strengths and weaknesses of divisions and support services and to assist in making decisions. Such self-audits are often conducted against the criteria of the Malcolm Baldrige National Quality Award. Some companies, such as AT&T, also have internal awards.

- Partnership with suppliers. They take steps to change from adversarial relationships with suppliers to partnerships. They shrink their supplier base by about two-thirds or more and require the surviving suppliers to take steps toward attaining world-class quality. They share information, and participate in planning improvement projects. Some even serve notice to the colleges which supply them with recruits: "If you want us to continue sending our recruiters to your campus, you will make the following quality improvements at your college."

- Business process quality management. They trace many quality problems to the business processes rather than factory processes. Often key business processes lack clear ownership. The steps in the process may have owners, but the overall process does not. Deeming this to be unacceptable, they assign owners to the key business processes, and spell out the responsibilities of owners. This results in dramatic improvements in customer service, error rates, productivity, time cycles, and costs.

- Self-directing teams. They train and empower workers to run processes with minimal help from supervisors or from specialists, such as process engineers. To make this work, they create self-directing teams. Jobs cross former functional lines; jobs become team jobs; workers become team members; quality and productivity improve; the ratio of workers to managers rises, as team members both plan and execute.

> ## Savvy Leadership
>
> To promote quality work at all levels, Juran suggests preparing exhibits that show how the product is used by customers so that every employee understands how the results of his or her job affect the customer—this show-and-tell process can be used to benefit both external and internal customers.

Human Obstacles to Quality

The obstacles that are removable by motivation include

1. *Unawareness.* People are not aware that they are creating quality problems.
2. *Competition in priorities.* People are unable to achieve quality because other goals that have higher priority get in the way.
3. *Suboptimization.* The achievement of quality locally gets in the way of overall quality.
4. *Cultural myths.* People hold certain sincere beliefs that are related to quality but that are not based on fact. These "myths" can be an obstacle to constructive efforts to achieve quality leadership.

In most companies, these obstacles have their origin in prior managerial practices. It is therefore important to avoid any atmosphere of blame. The emphasis should be on what to do differently, and on the methods for making the needed changes.

Stephen R. Covey

1932–

*P*opular self-help and motivational guru, Stephen Covey, wrote the best-selling book, The 7 Habits of Highly Effective People, and has conducted seminars for many of the Fortune 500 companies. After earning a business administration degree from the University of Utah, he went to England for two years as a Mormon missionary. Upon return, Covey earned an MBA from Harvard University and then went to Ireland on another mission. After three years, he returned to become assistant to the president of Brigham Young University. There, he started teaching and earned a Ph.D. in business and education in 1976. Seven years later, he founded the Covey Leadership Center, with his focus on developing personal integrity and character within others, a central prerequisite to personal success.

Ten Keys to Transformation

1. Transformation starts with increased awareness of the need for change. We need an increased awareness of where we are in relation to where we want to be. We can't be in a state of denial about the need for change or about the kind of commitment and effort that it will take. Often increased aware-

ness comes from 360-degree feedback that makes denial difficult and from a stakeholder information and accountability system that drives the transformation process.

2. The next step is to enter into a "co-missioning" process, aligning your personal mission with the mission of your organization. This "co-missioning" is best done through involvement and participation. People must decide for themselves what impact the change will have on them and their sphere of influence. When your people share the same mission, you then have the natural reinforcement in the culture to perpetuate change.

3. Build a sense of internal security. The less internal security people have, the less they can adapt to external reality. They have to have some sense that the ground will not shift on them. If they try to get predictability out of structure and systems, they only create bureaucracy-fossilized organizations that are incapable of adapting quickly to shifts in the marketplace. People won't willingly change unless their security lies within. If their security lies outside themselves, they see change as a threat. We need a sense of permanency and security. Living on unstable ground all the time is like living through an earthquake every day.

4. You next have to make change legitimate at the personal level. If you give people a profound learning experience on listening with empathy, for example, the next day they can do something about it. But if you ask them to do something the day before, they'll rebel against it. They might say: "What are you trying to do? What's wrong with the way we are doing it now?" People must acknowledge:

"I need something that I don't have now." And they know that it won't come by just hoping for it and envisioning it. It involves a change in mind-set and skill set. They must pay the price in a development process to get it.

5. Take personal responsibility for results. Executives and employees often debate the question, "How much of that development should be the duty of the organization, and how much the role and responsibility of the individual?" I think that in the last analysis, competency is up to the individual. The individual should say, "The organization is a resource to me. I can draw upon this resource or go to other resources. If the organization proves not to be a resource to me, then I will have to get the knowledge, skills, and training on my own."

But if we look at training from the chief executive's point of view, I would say: "Yes, the individual is ultimately responsible, but we need to create a supportive environment and provide some resources to help people develop the competency that we need to be competitive." Many governments now give tax credits for training and development to encourage companies to invest in the health of the "goose" that lays the golden eggs.

6. Bury the old. Often there needs to be a "baptism"—a symbolic burial of the old body and taking up of a new body, new name, new position, new place, new language, and a new spirit. This symbolizes not that you have rejected the old, but that you are building upon the old and moving forward. I have seen this done very successfully where people get together and bury the old practices and old ways and all of the guilt associated with them. It becomes a

transition time. In her book *Passages,* Gail Sheehy writes: "Like the lobster, we, too, must shed a protective structure with each passage from one stage of human growth to the next. We are left exposed and vulnerable—but also yeasty and embryonic again, capable of stretching in ways we hadn't known before."

These times of passage also become something that people can look at and laugh about. If they don't take themselves so seriously, they can say: "We'll be making changes the rest our lives. This change process is not a one-shot deal."

7. Embrace the new way with a spirit of adventure. The very process of changing has to change. First, the organization should be centered on natural laws and enduring principles, because those laws are going to operate, regardless. You can't transform a politicized workplace into a quality culture unless you build on principles; otherwise, you won't have the foundation to support reform initiatives.

Principle-centered leaders create a common vision and seek to decrease the restraining forces. Profit-centered leaders often try to increase the driving forces. Temporarily they can make improvements, but these create tensions—and those tensions break out in new problems, requiring new driving forces. Performance dips as people become fatigued and cynical. Management by drives will lead to management by crises.

8. Be open to new options. Major change requires a spirit of adventure since you are in unknown territory. You don't know what will happen or what hand you are going to be dealt, but you are excited to discover what it is so you can appropriately respond to it.

I suggest that you enter into a negotiation or a transformation saying, "Let's begin with the end in mind. The end in mind is that we will have a solution that will be better than what either of us now proposes. We do not know what the end will be. It is something that we will work out between us. Synergy is what we seek. Having an open mind will give us more of an immunity to dichotomous, either-or thinking. So the next time we run into a problem with each other, we can go for something better—a third alternative." If the "end in mind" is more of a spirit or philosophy or relationship than it is a specific outcome, you can be open to new options.

9. Seek synergy with other stakeholders. I was visiting with a CEO the other day, helping him prepare an important speech in which he wanted to deal with the "worsening relationships" inside the organization. I suggested to him that strained relationships are often symptomatic of deeper ills inside the culture—ills such as the spirit of contention and the spirit of adversarialism in the way people solve their problems. I showed the CEO how the habits of interdependency, empathy, and synergy represent a way to deal with difficult issues and still maintain good working relationships. He said, "The other day, I met with an adversary, and said, 'Let's let the spirit of synergy be the spirit of our interaction with each other.' He agreed, and our meeting was fruitful! I was thrilled, but now we are back to our old fighting stances."

I said, "Why don't you be the model of the concept that we solve our problems through synergy. If the trust isn't sufficient for synergy, at least you can have a respectful compromise. But no more name calling or labeling. Set yourself up as the model, and if you falter, acknowledge it by saying, 'I have faltered in the past, and I may falter in the future, but I will acknowledge it in order to set a new pattern of civil dialogue inside our organization.' "

An appreciation of diversity allows for synergy, and synergy creates transformation. When people feel understood and valued, they can transform in their own way instead of according to some norm, clone, or mandate. The chief characteristic of cancer is that it makes all cells the same. It robs them of what makes them unique.

10. The key thing is the transcendent purpose. Today, we are so buried by private and special interests that we don't share a transcendent purpose. The other day, as I met with a group of military generals, I noticed that it was much more difficult for them to create mission statements in peace time as opposed to war time. They're more focused when they have an "enemy." But most turf battles block transformation because you're too concerned about protecting your special interests to have the incentive and motivation to transform. When you see the world in terms of "us versus them," you get into transacting, not transforming.

Extreme Measures

Imagine your funeral, Covey suggests, and there are to be four speakers: a family member, a friend, a work associate, and a member from your community. Imagine what character traits and what achievements you would want each of them to talk about. Now live it.

Transformation of people and organizations happens faster once we have shared awareness and pain. We can then bury the old and get on with the new without carrying all the baggage of "what-might-have-been" deals and "us-versus-them" relationships. Effective leaders "transform" people and organizations—changing them in mind and heart; enlarging vision, insight, mind and understanding; clarifying purposes; making behavior congruent with beliefs, principles, or values; and bringing about permanent, self-perpetuating, and bringing about momentum-building changes.

The Seven Habits of Highly Effective People

1. Be Proactive
   "It means more than merely taking initiative. It means that as human beings, we are responsible for our own lives."
2. Begin with the End in Mind
   "It's based on *imagination*—the ability to envision, to see the potential . . . If you want to have a successful enterprise, you clearly define what you're trying to accomplish."
3. Put First Things First
   "Effective management is putting first things first. While leadership decides what 'first things' are, it is management that puts them first, day-by-day, moment-by-moment. Management is discipline, carrying it out."
4. Think Win/Win
   "Win/Win is a frame of mind and heart that constantly seeks mutual benefit in all human interactions."

(Continued)

---

5. Seek First to Understand, then to Be Understood
   "When we really, deeply understand each other, we open the door to creative solutions and third alternatives. Our differences are no longer stumbling blocks to communication and progress."
6. Synergize
   "The essence of synergy is to value differences—to respect them, to build on strengths, to compensate for weaknesses."
7. Sharpen the Saw
   "It's preserving and enhancing the greatest asset you have—you. It's renewing the four dimensions of your nature—physical, spiritual, mental, and social/emotional."

PART VII

~

Builders of Culture

Ben Cohen and Jerry Greenfield

1951– , 1951–

*E*very ice cream connoisseur knows Ben and Jerry, who are *famous for their wild flavors and social activism. They met in a high school gym class in their Long Island hometown, and realized they shared a love for food, not athletics. In 1969, they went their separate ways to college, with Ben eventually failing to become a potter and Jerry failing to get into medical school. In 1977, they reunited to start their own business. They mulled over bagels and pizza, but settled on making ice cream where there was little competition: Burlington, Vermont. Ben and Jerry, whose aspirations include building a community as opposed to just a workplace, were cowinners of the 1988 National Small Business Person of the Year Award. It was presented to them by President Ronald Reagan, even though the two were campaigning against Reagan's military buildup.*

Our Aspirations

TO BE REAL: We need to be who we say we are, both inside and outside the company. We are all custodians of the reputation of Ben & Jerry's. We will strive to put into practice the words we use to describe ourselves: Friendly, Enthusiastic, Exciting, Caring, High-Quality, Progressive, Off-beat, Innovative, Cutting-Edge, Funny, Lighthearted, Encouraging, Informal, Activist, Honest, Childlike, Down-Home.

TO BE THE BEST: If our customers are euphoric about our products, we will prosper. Our future together depends upon our ability to outperform the competition. That's our business strategy. We want to be the best ice cream company in the world. We want to be viewed as master ice cream makers. We are passionate about giving customers what they want, when they want it, every single time.

TO IMPROVE CONTINUOUSLY: Every time we do something, we should be checking to see if our methods worked and figure out how we can do it better the next time. From the minute we join the company we are responsible for helping to shape and improve what goes on around us.

TO LEARN CONTINUOUSLY: We want people to have the opportunity to develop their potential to contribute to the company. We'll need to keep growing skills in three areas: technical skills to achieve excellence in day-to-day work, personal skills to give life and vitality to these aspirations, and business knowledge to understand the companywide implications and importance of what each of us does.

TO BE INCLUSIVE: We embrace individual differences. The right to be ourselves contributes to our sense of ownership. We perform better and serve the marketplace better when men, women, gays, lesbians, and people of different races, nationalities, ethnicities, and backgrounds work together. Building a diverse staff contributes to excellent performance, not just to societal good.

To Be Creative: Our creativity is our strength. We want to see beyond conventional thinking and come up with ideas that work, that excite our customers and reflect our values.

To Build Community: No one at Ben & Jerry's should feel alone or apart. When one of us needs help, we reach out to help. People from outside feel our energy when they visit us. We have a zest for life, a sense of humor, and we enjoy one another's company. We share the excitement of succeeding at the game of business and we'll try to have fun while we do it.

To Be Open and Trusting: Rationales, strategy, and the truth should be shared. We want to be open about our concerns and admit our mistakes and failings. We need to make sure people feel safe to speak up about things they

> ### Outrageous Promotion
>
> To promote ice cream sales in winter, the twosome would take a penny off the cost of a cone for every degree below 0°C, otherwise known as Penny Off Per Celsius Degree Below Zero Winter Extravaganza, or POPCDBZWE. Because their first store was located in Burlington, Vermont, the promotion turned a liability (the cold weather) into an asset.

care about. If we trust one another's good intentions, we'll feel better about trying new things and about speaking up about things that concern us. It's expected that we'll all do the right thing even when nobody is looking.

To Celebrate and to Give Meaningful Recognition: When we reach or exceed our targets, we should cheer. Celebration establishes a sense of accomplishment, which leads to more accomplishments. Celebrations don't need to be elaborate. Recognition is the currency of leadership. We should make recognition a contagious part of everyday life.

To Use Consultive Decision Making and Active Listening: When making decisions we'll involve people with special expertise and people likely to be affected. We'll also give those with a contrary point of view an opportunity to be heard. However, Ben & Jerry's is not a democracy. Leaders need to make calls based on facts, data, and input. In order to practice consultive decision making and to create the conditions for people to contribute their best thinking, we must be active listeners.

To Hold Ourselves Accountable: We all need to do what we said we were going to do and be clear about who's responsible and what's expected. When we don't do our part it affects everybody. We put the company at risk when we tolerate poor performance.

To Be Great Communicators: Leaders are responsible for effectively and consistently communicating pertinent information in a timely way. Good leaders have well-informed teams. We're each responsible for absorbing the information offered through company communication vehicles like postings, staff meetings, and *The Rolling Cone.*

To Be Up-Front: People aren't going to do better unless they understand what they need to do to improve. Good straight feedback is essential to improvement. Talking about someone's performance to people other than the person does harm to the individual and to the company.

To Be Profitable by Being Thrifty: We believe in investing wisely and with a sense of frugality. When we save the company money, we do a service to our shareholders and ourselves.

Ben and Jerry's Social Mission Statement

We have a progressive, nonpartisan social agenda.
We seek peace by supporting nonviolent ways to resolve conflict.
We will look for ways to create economic opportunities for the disenfranchised.
We are committed to practicing caring capitalism.
We seek to minimize our negative impact on the environment.
We support family farming and sustainable methods of food production.

Howard M. Schultz

1953–

*A*s CEO of Starbucks, the international chain of coffee bars, Howard Schultz put romance back in the coffee bean. He grew up in Brooklyn, where his blue-collar family struggled to make ends meet. Fortunately, Schultz won a football scholarship to Northern Michigan University. After earning a business degree in 1975, he became a sales rep for Xerox, and two jobs later joined Seattle-based Starbucks (then just a coffee bean wholesaler) in 1982. After four years, Schultz left the company to start a chain of coffee bars, only to buy Starbucks in 1987 for $3.8 million. He took the company public in 1992 and, as of 1999, the company was operating more than 2,800 stores around the world. Success has depended upon Schultz never compromising his principles when it comes to coffee quality and store atmosphere.

Starbucks Mission Statement

Establish Starbucks as the premier purveyor of the finest coffee in the world while maintaining our uncompromising principles as we grow. The following six guiding principles will help us measure the appropriateness of our decisions:

Provide a great work environment and treat
each other with respect and dignity.

Embrace diversity as an essential component
in the way we do business.

Apply the highest standards of
excellence to the purchasing,
roasting, and fresh delivery
of our coffee.

Develop enthusiastically
satisfied customers all
of the time.

Smart Habits

On the way to work, Schultz stops by one of several dozen Seattle-area Starbucks for a cup of java; it jump-starts his day and keeps him in touch with the front lines.

Contribute positively to our communities
and our environment.

Recognize that profitability is essential
to our future success.

Capturing the Customer's Imagination

A taste of romance. At Starbucks stores, people get a five-
or ten-minute break that takes them far from the routine of their daily lives. Where else can you go to get a
whiff of Sumatra or Kenya or Costa Rica? Where else
can you get a taste of Verona or Milan? Just having the
(Continued)

chance to order a drink as exotic as an *espresso mac-chiato* adds a spark of romance to an otherwise unre-markable day.

An affordable luxury. In our stores you may see a police-man or a utility worker standing in line in front of a wealthy surgeon. The blue-collar man may not be able to afford the Mercedes the surgeon just drove up in, but he can order the same $2.00 cappuccino. They're both giving themselves a reward and enjoying some-thing world class.

An oasis. In an increasingly fractured society, our stores offer a quiet moment to gather your thoughts and cen-ter yourself. Starbucks people smile at you, serve you quickly, don't harass you. A visit to Starbucks can be a small escape during a day when so many other things are beating you down. We've become a breath of fresh air.

Casual social interaction. One of the advertising agencies that pitched for our business interviewed Los Angeles–area customers in focus groups. The common thread among their comments was this: "Starbucks is so social. We go to Starbucks stores because of a social feeling."

John Wanamaker

1838–1922

*J*ohn Wanamaker was a pioneer of the modern department store, involved and innovative right up until his final years—he also had quite a reputation for filling notebooks full of maxims in the spirit of Ben Franklin. At age 13, he went to work as an errand boy for a publishing house, earning $1.25 a week. Not long after that, he joined a men's clothing business and rose to salesman, but was then hired by the Philadelphia chapter of the Young Men's Christian Association in 1857. Four years later, Wanamaker and his brother-in-law had saved enough money to buy their own men's clothing business, and then Wanamaker opened his own shop in 1869. It was another seven years until he bought an old freight depot and converted it into "a new kind of store"—a collection of specialty shops under one roof that evolved into today's department store.

The Knows, the Keeps, the Takes, the Gives

Know yourself.
Know your merchandise.
Know how to present yourself and your merchandise.
Keep your mind on your work.
Keep sweet.

Keep listening to your customer rather than talking yourself.

Keep wide awake to effect the sales.

Keep steady at each transaction until goods are wrapped and on the way to delivery.

Take care to be accurate.

Take trouble to be punctual and prompt.

Extreme Measures

To force himself to save money, little by little, Wanamaker took out 62 life insurance policies. (At age 50, he was more insured than any other American; at age 57, his policies were worth more than $1.5 million.)

Take pains to spell back the name, number, street and town of the addresses given you.

Take no offence under any circumstances.

Take firm hold of anything that displeases a customer and set it right before leaving it.

Take sufficient time to avoid mistakes.

Give sufficient care to suit the customer, so that goods will stay sold.

Smart Habits

To enliven his advertising copy, which he personally wrote, Wanamaker studied the dictionary and made his own collection of the most interesting words.

Give yourself a little rest between customers, if possible.

Give a call to the medical director, at his office, if in the least sick, so that you will quickly mend a cold and not have to be absent when the store needs you.

Dave Thomas

1932–

A s an adopted child who moved 12 times in 15 years, the founder of Wendy's restaurant chain only knew work to be a "constant companion." During the Korean War, he volunteered and attended the army's Cook and Baker School. Feeding 2,000 hungry soldiers a day taught him "some important skills about the big picture of feeding a lot of people." After the army, he worked as a short-order cook for a man who owned four Kentucky Fried Chicken franchises. The franchises were failing, so Thomas was offered a deal: If he could turn around the KFCs, he would get 45 percent ownership. He made good and then cashed out for $1 million in 1968 to start Wendy's. Thomas, who appears in the company's humorous and disarming TV commercials, enjoys razzing his people to keep them on their toes.

Dave's Rules for Successful Harassment

1. **Make sure people trust you.** I remember when Denny Lynch, our vice president of communications, first started working for us. Denny was so intense, I kept on harassing him to get him to loosen up. One day, I teased him to the brink, and he shot back, "Mr. Thomas, are you questioning my veracity?" I said, "I don't know." Then, I teased him for

three more days for using a word I didn't understand. The more I saw Denny, the more uptight he looked. Finally, it dawned on me that Denny didn't trust me. He thought that since I was always on his case I was one step away from canning him. That wasn't my idea at all. Later I read something in a book called *Leaders* by Warren Bennis and Burt Nanus that stuck with me. In it, they say that Los Angeles Rams coach John Robinson "never criticizes his players until they're convinced of his unconditional confidence in their abilities." That's a good outlook to have.

As for Denny and harassment, he's totally sold on the program now. The other day, I overheard him talking to another guy I'd been badgering. "Don't worry," Denny said. "If he's harassing you, it means he likes you. If he didn't think you could take it or that you were a zero, he wouldn't say a thing."

2. **Start early.** I first met Charlie Rath, our executive vice president of marketing, in 1977. He had just "sold" Wendy's on being the local sponsor for Grand Prix Tennis—the Columbus stop on the professional tennis circuit. Every time I saw Charlie I would ask him when the signs would go up to let people know about the event. Finally, we were getting pretty close to the day the matches would start. Charlie maintained it was about three months before the tournament. I said three days. It was probably more like three weeks. Well, Charlie finally went out and did something. He had a bunch of signs screen-printed and nailed one on each of the nearly five hundred telephone poles between my house and the tennis stadium.

3. **Tell people when they're almost perfect . . . but do it nice.** When Charlie finally got the signs up, I made sure that I

thanked him for the great job. Then I gave him a slip of paper with the addresses of the two phone poles he missed.

4. **Make 'em feel guilty when they do nothing.** One thing I can't stand is people who don't act on a situation. I'd rather that people make mistakes than sit around and not do something.

5. **Don't put up with excuses.** Poor results are bad enough, but weak excuses are even worse. I visit about fifty different markets each year to see Wendy's operations. When I'm on the road, I'll visit as many restaurants as I can.

Extreme Measures

Thomas believes most entrepreneurs get into trouble by offering too many products; so Wendy's, with its down-home atmosphere, kept the exact same limited menu of hamburgers, chili, french fries, Frosty shakes, and various beverages for 10 years.

Most of the time, I'm happy with what we see, but sometimes not. Nothing makes me more unhappy than when I get weak excuses and alibis to explain poor performance. So, I always try to go easier on bad performance than when somebody is punting or lying.

6. **Don't let up until they go out there and find out.** Whenever our marketing people come in and tell me about somebody else's new sandwich, the first thing I'll ask is, "Did ya try it?" If somebody comes up with a new store design, I want to know what it looks like in real life. The same thing goes for problems inside your business. You can get all the reports in the world — most of them written to cover up what the real problems are — but there is no substitute for going out there and nosing around yourself.

You've got to be real careful when you harass people. I just don't think harassment works for managers who are not perceived as nice people by their team. And if people don't know you like them and you start harassing them, they'll just clam up on you or even serve you a knuckle sandwich. But harassment can work. Why? So much of any business is detail and execution, and any manager has to stay on top of it. Harassment is personal communications. It's not some dumb, dull memo that you could just as well address "To Whom It May Concern."

Smart Habits

Every month, Wendy's polls 500 customers to see what they think of the menu, food quality, and the restaurant itself.

7. ***Batch things for people.*** People tell me that I always have a bunch of lists going on in my head with messages for people. I'm a laundry list type of guy, and I've been blessed with a pretty good memory. When I see somebody, I try to go through my whole list with them. It's really just "packaging," and it's a lot better than writing a bunch of stupid memos. It's not much different from what you do with your kids as they go sailing out the door: "When did you say you were going to clean the basement? The cat's not happy with the litter box . . . and don't forget your galoshes."

8. ***Make harassment fun.*** Businesses focus too much on "productivity" and too little on fun. I've made more money by having fun than I have not having fun. That would be true for most people, if they gave themselves the chance. A little well-meant harassment is the best way I know to connect hard work and having fun. To me the perfect employee is someone who has fun doing the job.

Mark McCormack

1930–

*I*t took only one client to put Mark McCormack on the road to becoming the most powerful person in sports—the legendary golfer Arnold Palmer, whom he signed in 1959. After earning an undergraduate degree at William & Mary, McCormack attended Yale's Law School and then joined a Cleveland, Ohio, law firm. Not long after, Palmer walked through the door looking for help. Realizing the opportunities that sports agenting and marketing presented, McCormack quit the law firm and founded the International Management Group (IMG) with $500 in start-up capital. Over the years, McCormack added a variety of characters to his stables, from the violinist Itzhak Perlman to tennis star Chris Evert to Tiger Woods, and the firm now has 76 offices in 31 countries. A key to his success has been developing honest relationships devoid of duplicity.

The Ten Most Toxic Lies in Business

The fact is, the workplace is a far healthier environment because of all the little lies that we allow to float harmlessly among us. I'm especially in favour of the white lies that spare other people's feelings, the ones where you don't say what you really think of their unfortunate haircuts or their ridiculous new glasses or their poorly researched reports. Why start a fight or bruise an ego when a few words of innocuous approval will suffice?

However, there is a wholly different sector of lies that are far less benign. These are the clichés and verbal mantras that many people employ to mask their failings at work. These catchphrases are hard to argue with, but you should perk up when you hear them because they often come out of the mouths of people who mean exactly the opposite of what they are saying. Here are 10 of the most common and therefore most dangerous lies in business:

1. "I can keep a secret."

    In my experience people who can keep a confidence don't brag about it because the alternative, namely betraying a confidence, is not an issue with them. People who tell you they can keep a secret invariably don't.

    This is similar to people who say, "I always meet my deadlines," or "I always deliver on time." Punctuality isn't an issue with people who are always on time. They take it for granted. It only matters to people who tend to miss their deadlines.

2. "This was a rational decision."

    People say this in order to take the personal sting out of a decision that will adversely affect you. As if a rational decision deserves a rational response from you. Don't be fooled. There are no perfectly rational decisions. Every decision, even that based on hard numbers, is a series of either/or choices that are founded as much on intuition or personal inclination as anything else. In other words "This was a rational decision" really means "I wanted to do this."

3. "I want totally honest feedback."

When bosses say "I want to know what you really think" they probably mean it. It's the moment after you tell them what you really think that the statement becomes a lie because they don't react to your blunt opinion in a welcoming manner. Whether they resent it or they're hurt by it or they don't believe it, very few are grateful to you for saying it. Consciously or not, they will usually punish you for it.

> ### Smart Habits
>
> McCormack has preferred waking up early enough to spend an hour reading, relaxing, and exercising, before getting ready for work—even if it means setting the alarm for 5:00 A.M. Result: no rushing around and no feeling that work imposes on personal time.

There are plenty of occasions to tell the boss the unvarnished truth. Ironically, when the boss asks for it is not one of them.

4. "The cheque is in the mail."

This is the grandaddy of business lies, so egregious and trite that people laugh about it as they are saying it. Of course the accompanying laugh track doesn't make this lie more palatable. When you hear this the truth is plain and simple: you have a collection problem.

5. "You're the only one we're talking to."

This is the lie about exclusivity. When people tell me I'm the only one they're talking to about a project they're probably telling the truth. What's missing from this sentence, however, is the phrase, ". . . but if things don't go our way we won't hesitate to talk to other people too."

There's nothing wrong with this. We're all adults in business. In any transaction I realize that I don't have the field all to myself. I just wish more people would state their real intentions.

6. "It's business. It's not personal."

You can thank The Godfather for this one.

The truth is everything is personal. All things being equal in business people won't shaft you if they personally like you. In fact they'll go out of their way to help a friend even when all things are less than equal. Likewise they won't hesitate to decide against you if there is no personal connection.

This phrase is not a lie so much as a contradiction. If it's business it only means that there was nothing significantly personal between you.

7. "The customer comes first."

Quite often this is true. But in even the noblest of service businesses people shade the truth. They're selective. They treat customers differently depending on what they think they can get away with. Big customers get taken care of because doing so clearly benefits the business. Little customers get ignored if people perceive there is little risk to their business.

8. "I'll call you right back."

This is more a verbal tic than a lie. People say it to end a phone conversation or because they have to take another call. Unless it

---

Smart Habits

To avoid interruptions in his workday, McCormack rarely takes a phone call. He also prefers to initiate the phone call so he can prepare what he wants to say and control the flow of conversation.

serves their interest to call back immediately, people rarely deliver on this promise.

If you're one of those people who are still waiting for the return call, you shouldn't.

9. "We judge people on their performance."

If this were true the workplace would be a perfect meritocracy. The truth is more like "We judge your performance based on how much we like you." People don't get fired for not doing their jobs well. They get canned because someone in authority doesn't like them. It's that simple.

10. "The boss is clueless."

This is more a myth than a lie. It's uttered by every subordinate who thinks he or she is smarter than their boss. It's also a convenient excuse when an unpopular decision needs explaining. Don't believe it. There are usually sounder reasons for an unpopular decision than the boss' purported ignorance.

Extreme Measures

If you want to get in with an *inaccessible* bigwig for business reasons, McCormack advises befriending a friend of the bigwig and then using your now mutual acquaintance as a reference to gain access

Rene C. McPherson

1924–

*R*ene McPherson *was a maverick CEO whose progressive management style at the Dana Corporation made him famous. After a stint in the USAAF, he earned a B.S. degree from Case Institute of Technology and an MBA from Harvard in 1952. He then joined Dana, an auto parts manufacturer with a strong international presence, eventually becoming CEO. The company was wallowing in bureaucracy, so he cut 350 people from a corporate staff of 500, decentralized operations, encouraged employees to participate in the Dana stock plan, and established Dana University (a premier in-house training program). In addition, McPherson, whose maverick policies created an extremely productive climate, oversaw the purchase of 24 companies from 1963 to 1980 to diversify and to improve the company's financial performance.*

Creating a Productive Climate

There are a few contributions toward a productive climate that are basic enough to fit any organizational application:

- *Nothing more effectively involves people, sustains credibility or generates enthusiasm than face-to-face communication. As a* total group, both within departments and on an individual basis, our people must meet regularly to discuss goals, objectives, financial performance, the status of suggestions, the future or whatever else is on their minds. I do not believe in corporate procedures; they are counterproductive and restrict the flexibility of people to respond to the unpredictable. They also retard the inventiveness, professional development and accountability of managers. Among the few corporate policies that must survive, however, is the one requiring managers and leaders to meet with *all* of their people regularly—to talk, to explain and to *listen*.

- *It is critical to provide and discuss all organizational performance figures with all of our people.* Bad news is as important as good news, and candor is essential. If we are managing well, our people have tough goals to meet, and they must know how they are doing as judged against performance yardsticks. Regular meetings help ensure that our goals are understood, and offer the opportunity to share the recognition for having met the challenges.

- *We have an obligation to provide training and the opportunity for development to our productive people who want to improve their skills, expand their career opportunities or simply further their general education.* Tailor the programs to their specific requirements and listen to their evaluations of those programs. Forget about trying to cost-justify education; rely instead on instinct. Everyone responds positively to needs that are, or can be, satisfied. Smart companies during the last recession used the period as an opportunity.

- *This is the most difficult: It is essential to provide job security for our people.* Concentrate on eliminating cyclitility and business fluctuation as well as on establishing an environment where layoffs and work shortages are not considered to be as inevitable as they once were. Most of our people are well insulated from the shock of a layoff to their earnings through a series of income-protection plans. But no matter how sheltered our people are by supplemental unemployment benefits, layoffs are bad. They create an attitude of uncertainty, disrupt productive programs, undermine our credibility and erode the spirit of optimism and aggressiveness so important in our work areas. They have the effect of saying to our people, "As hard as you work, and as valuable as your ideas are, we don't need you right now." We do need them, and we need to correct situations that cause employment interruptions. It takes excellent leaders and exceptional long-term planning to accomplish this.

> ### *Extreme Measures*
>
> When McPherson became CEO, he replaced 17-inch-thick company manuals with concise policy statements, put an end to management reports that generated over 400 pages each month, terminated the use of memos for communication so managers would meet face-to-face, and removed all time clocks from their facilities.

• *Create incentive programs that rely on ideas and suggestions, as well as on hard work, to establish a reward pool.* Then distribute this pool as a percent of income to *everyone* in the particular operation, without respect to rank. Group cohesion is vital.

I learned years ago that most organizations are too large to be run from one office or through the sheer dynamism of a few individuals. I also learned that if we do not listen to our people, encourage them to participate and recognize the immense talent they have, we shall fall short of our growth expectations and our obligation to provide our constituencies the performance they expect.

Mary Kay Ash

*M*ary Kay Ash is perhaps best recognized by the pink car
she awards top cosmetics saleswomen. Ash, who infuses
her management philosophy with the Golden Rule, attributes
her success to her mother. While growing up in Texas, her father
suffered from tuberculosis and her mother supported the family.
Subsequently, Ash had more than her share of household chores,
so her mother encouraged her with the mantra: "You can do it."
After working 11 years as a sales rep for Stanley Home Products,
Ash quit to start her own business when a male assistant, who'd
been with the company less than two years, became her boss.
Unfortunately, a month before Mary Kay Cosmetics was to open
in 1963, her husband had a fatal heart attack and all seemed
lost. She later reflected, however, "No matter what anyone
thought, I just couldn't give up my dream."

Treat People Fairly

Solving management problems by applying the Golden Rule
means treating people fairly and according to merit, not
merely using them for self-serving purposes. To some this
seems in conflict with a company's profit motive; I think, however, the two can be harmonious. For instance, a person may

ask for an unreasonably high increase in salary, one that does not give the company a fair return for services rendered. "My wife lost her job, and we have two kids in college," an employee may plead; "I need a raise." A good manager will be sympathetic, but he can't always comply with even the most justifiable wants and needs of his employees. In order to balance responsibilities to the company, the employee, and all other employees, every manager must be able to say no.

I understand that this can be unpleasant. But instead of approaching the job as a task to be endured—I try to turn it into a positive situation. I want that employee to turn a "no" into the motivation for accomplishing more. And I do this with four simple steps.

> ### Extreme Measures
> Ash wrote her goals on her bathroom mirror at home, so that she would have to face them every morning.

1. It is imperative that each employee be confident that no decision will be arbitrary. And so the first thing I do is to listen and then restate the question. This reassures the employee that I do indeed understand the scope of his problem.
2. I clearly list the logical reasons why his request cannot be granted.
3. I give a direct "no" statement. This is so important if you are to build trust and respect among people. It's not fair to expect someone else to surmise or guess your real intent.
4. And finally I try to suggest how the employee's goal may be reached by some other path. For example, to this hypothetical employee I might say, "Bill, I am truly sorry about

your wife's misfortune. But you know, she may be on the threshold of a whole new career. This could be your opportunity to help her discover her real talents. God didn't have time to make a nobody; we all have the capacity for greatness. Why don't you sit down with her tonight and talk about what she would really like to accomplish next?"

Smart Habits

Whether speaking with a work associate or a friend, Ash espouses looking them directly in the eye at all times—a wandering eye equates to a wandering mind.

A good manager will confront problems of this nature with sensitivity and seek the best solutions. But the solutions cannot compromise his responsibility to his company or to other people within the organization.

Establishing Yourself

- Always be *truthful* with your employees. If they ask for information you cannot reveal, say so. If they ask something that you don't know—say that as well. Most people are very quick to discern a smoke screen.
- Be *consistent* in facts and attitude. Not only will this help employees understand you, but it will also allow them to function with security.
- Be *relaxed* and *confident* when dealing with others. Even something as obvious as using a calm tone of voice can put

your employees at ease. Think things through before you say them (be certain you are saying what you mean) and be yourself.

- Whenever possible, *use "we" instead of "I"* when discussing your people with others. Word will definitely get back that you accept and respect their contributions.
- Finally, always *remember where you came from,* and bear in mind that your future in management depends upon your ability to work well with people. While pomp is something that fascinates all of us on occasion, pomposity is never admirable—least of all in a manager.

Thomas J. Watson, Jr.

1914–1993

*B*ack *in 1987, Fortune magazine selected IBM CEO Thomas Watson as "the greatest capitalist in history." Yet, while growing up he was known as "Terrible Tom;" in prep school he tried marijuana; and he barely graduated from Brown University. Watson was commissioned a second lieutenant in the air force, and quickly learned how to manage the men under his command during World War II. He realized "that I had the force of personality to get my ideas across to others." After the war, Watson was prepared to work as a pilot for United Air Lines, but his commanding general convinced him to return to IBM, where he'd been in sales before the war. He quickly rose through the ranks, became president in 1952, and succeeded his father as chairman in 1956. It was a period of tumultuous change, but Watson succeeded by focusing on good old human relations.*

What Growth and Change Have Taught Us

In looking back on the history of a company, one can't help but reflect on what the organization has learned from its years in business. In thinking specifically of the period since the war when IBM faced the twin challenges of great technological change and growth, I would say that we've come out with five key lessons. They may not be applicable to all companies. All I can do is attest to the great value these five lessons had for us.

1. There is simply no substitute for good human relations and for the high morale they bring. It takes good people to do the jobs necessary to reach your profit goals. But good people alone are not enough. No matter how good your people may be, if they don't really like the business, if they don't feel

> ### Savvy Leadership
>
> Never hesitate to promote someone you don't like, Watson advised. He preferred scratchy, harsh, unpleasant folks who told it like it was. If a promoted lieutenant erred, Watson put him/her in his so-called penalty box, which amounted to a boring job off the fast track, until they redeemed themselves.

totally involved in it, or if they don't think they're being treated fairly—it's awfully hard to get a business off the ground. Good human relations are easy to talk about. The real lesson, I think, is that you must work at them all the time and make sure your managers are working with you.

2. There are two things an organization must increase far out of proportion to its growth rate if that organization is to overcome the problems of change. The first of these is communication, upward and downward. The second is education and retraining.

3. Complacency is the most natural and insidious disease of large corporations. It can be overcome if management will set the right tone and pace and if its lines of communication are in working order.

4. Everyone—particularly in a company such as IBM—must place company interest above that of a division or depart-

ment. In an interdependent organization, a community of effort is imperative. Cooperation must outrank self-interest, and an understanding of the company's particular approach to things is more important than technical ability.

5. And the final and most important lesson: Beliefs must always come before policies, practices, and goals. The latter must always be altered if they are seen to violate fundamental beliefs. The only sacred cow in an organization should be its basic philosophy of doing business.

The British economist Walter Bagehot once wrote: "Strong beliefs win strong men and then make them stronger." To this I would add, "And as men become stronger, so do the organizations to which they belong."

PART VIII

∼

Maxims for Life

Al Neuharth

1924–

*W*hen the future founder of USA Today and Gannett chairman was only 22 months old, his dad died, and at age 10, Neuharth took a newspaper delivery job at 12 cents a week to help fill the family coffers. In high school, he first pursued journalism, and he was editor of the school's paper in his senior year. After serving in World War II, he studied at the University of South Dakota (his home state), and then cofounded SoDak Sports, a newspaper that was dedicated to sports. It folded after two years. Neuharth, who merrily refers to himself as an S.O.B., went on to work for the Miami Herald and the Detroit Free Press, and was eventually offered the job of managing two of the Gannett's 16 papers. Neuharth lived by his own rules, which included how to avoid burnout, and eventually became Gannett's chairman, launching USA Today in 1982.

An S.O.B.'s Ten Secrets to Success

- Expect others to do unto you what you would do unto them.
- Somebody wants something you have. Protect it.
- Somebody has something you want. Go for it.
- Be as nice as possible, only as nasty as necessary.
- Treasure your family and your roots but never turn back.

Outrageous Promotion

To ensure that he received a standing ovation when it came time to announce the launch of *USA Today* to 400 Gannett executives, Neuharth had a few allies placed strategically throughout the crowd with instructions to start the "spontaneous standing ovation" at the right moment.

- Explore the byways as well as the highways of life.
- Think Big. Big dreams. Big risks. Big rewards.
- Scramble to the top and don't tiptoe while you're there.
- Bow out while all your marbles are still intact.
- Life's a game. Play it to win. And to enjoy.

How to Avoid Burnout

Whether at home or away, I take care of myself.

Executives who pride themselves on hard work but ignore fun and fitness are candidates for career burnout.

People ask me why I appear so relaxed after a long day of work or days of travel: It's simple. Be very particular about what you put into your body and how you use it. You too can feel great if you:

- Eat only when you're hungry.
- Drink only when you're thirsty.
- Sleep only when you're tired.
- Screw only when you're horny.

There may be more scientific ways to achieve fun and fitness in a first-class way, but I haven't found them yet.

Kemmons Wilson

1913–

K emmons Wilson, founder of Holiday Inns and father of the modern hotel, was just nine months old when his own father died. To help support the family, he dropped out of high school and worked as a stock boy for a cotton broker, and then he built up a pinball machine franchise. During the Great Depression, he bought cheap property and built homes. The idea for a motel chain came to him when he drove his family from Memphis to Washington, D.C. in 1951—motel choices were limited and not kid-friendly. Beginning in 1952, he built four motels around Memphis, just off the highways to cater to travelers. When Wilson retired in 1979, there were 1,759 Holiday Inns in 50 countries—the result of his down-to-earth beliefs that draw upon a positive mental attitude.

Twenty Tips for Success

1. Work only a half a day; it makes no difference which half—it can be either the first 12 hours or the last 12 hours.
2. Work is the master key that opens the door to all opportunities.

3. Mental attitude plays a far more important role in a person's success or failure than mental capacity.
4. Remember that we all climb the ladder of success one step at a time.
5. There are two ways to get to the top of an oak tree. One way is to sit on an acorn and wait; the other way is to climb it.
6. Do not be afraid of taking a chance. Remember that a broken watch is exactly right at least twice every 24 hours.
7. The secret of happiness is not in doing what one likes, but in liking what one does.
8. Eliminate from your vocabulary the words, "I don't think I can" and substitute, "I know I can."
9. In evaluating a career, put opportunity ahead of security.
10. Remember that success requires half luck and half brains.
11. A person has to take risks to achieve.

> ### Smart Habits
> To save time while on the road, at restaurants Wilson would order and eat his dessert while waiting for his main course.

12. People who take pains never to do more than they get paid for, never get paid for anything more than they do.
13. No job is too hard as long as you are smart enough to find someone else to do it for you.
14. Opportunity comes often. It knocks as often as you have an ear trained to hear it, an eye trained to see it, a hand trained to grasp it, and a head trained to use it.
15. You cannot procrastinate—in two days, tomorrow will be yesterday.
16. Sell your wristwatch and buy an alarm clock.

17. A successful person realizes his personal responsibility for self-motivation. He starts himself because he possesses the key to his own ignition switch.

18. Do not worry. You can't change the past, but you sure can ruin the present by worrying over the future. Remember that half the things we worry about never happen, and the other half are going to happen anyway. So, why worry?

> ### *Extreme Measures*
> To find great hotel locations, Wilson flew his own plane—often upside down for a better view—and more than once almost crashed in his excitement.

19. It is not how much you have but how much you enjoy that makes happiness.

20. Believe in God and obey the Ten Commandments.

Carley Fiorina

1954–

$\mathcal{A}$ s the first outsider to be named CEO of Hewlett-Packard (HP), Carley Fiorina has her work cut out. Founded by William Hewlett and Dave Packard in 1938 in a Palo Alto garage, HP is considered the birthplace of Silicon Valley, and has a rich and staid culture that tends to resist change. After graduating from Stanford University in 1976 with degrees in medieval history and philosophy, Fiorina taught English in Italy. She then received an MBA from the University of Maryland and subsequently joined AT&T. Fiorina, who has a reputation for dogged determination and clear vision, helped execute the Lucent Technologies spin-off in 1996 and was named chief of Lucent's $20 billion Global Service Provider business. HP recruited her in 1999, and at that time, she became one of only three women running Fortune 500 companies.

Seven Principles for Personal and Business Growth

- Recognize the power of the team; no one succeeds alone.

- "Never, never, never, never give in," to quote Winston Churchill. Most great wins happen on the last play.

- Strike a balance between confidence and humility—enough confidence to know that you can make a real difference, enough humility to ask for help.

- Love what you do. Success requires passion.

- Seek tough challenges: they're more fun.

Savvy Leadership

After giving a speech to employees, Fiorina shouts, "Send me 'The 10 Stupidest Things We Do!' I'll read it!"

- Have an unflinching, clear-eyed vision of the goal, followed by absolute clarity, realism and objectivity about what it really will take to grow, to lead and to win.

- Understand that the only limits that really matter are those you put on yourself, or that a business puts on itself. Most people and businesses are capable of far more than they realize.

Conrad Hilton

1887–1971

*T*he founder of the Hilton Hotels Corporation knew both poverty and glamour: Conrad Hilton grew up in New Mexico in the same "primitive adobe" that housed his father's general store; he later married and divorced Zsa Zsa Gabor and became the proud owner of the Waldorf-Astoria. After attending the New Mexico School of Mines for two years and serving in the army during World War I, Hilton desperately wanted to be an independent banker. An old friend advised him to seek his fortune in Texas, because where there's oil there's action. When Hilton tried to find a hotel bed his first night in Texas, he couldn't and he knew immediately what to buy—not a bank, but a hotel. Hilton was always a big dreamer who refused to cling to the past, two elements he lists in his art for living.

There Is an Art to Living

Find Your Own Particular Talent: As surely as none of us was given the exact same thumb print, so surely none of us possesses the exact same talent. This does not mean there will not be two housewives, two carpenters, two artists or two hotel men.

We each have two thumbs. But the individual print is uniquely our own.

Emerson says, "Each man has his own vocation. The talent is the call . . . He inclines to do something which is easy for him, and good when it is done, but which no other man can do . . . His ambition is exactly proportioned to his powers. The height of the pinnacle is determined by the breadth of the base."

Finding this particular talent or vocation is the first step in the art of successful living. Great frustration and the *feel* of failure can be present in the face of material success if we follow someone else's footsteps rather than our own. . . .

Be Big: Think Big. Act Big. Dream Big.

Your value is determined by the mold you yourself make. It doesn't take any more energy to expect to be the best housewife, the finest cook, the most capable carpenter.

It has been my experience that the way most people court failure is by misjudging their abilities, belittling their worth and value. Did you ever think what can happen to a plain bar of iron, worth about $5.00? The same iron when made into horseshoes is worth $10.50. If made into needles, it is worth $3,750.85, and if turned into balance springs for watches its value jumps to $250,000.

The same is true of another kind of material — You! . . .

Be Honest: What I have in mind is something more than the negative virtues of not cheating, not lying, not stealing. It is a bold, direct, open stand for the truth as we know it, both to ourselves and others. My mother had two old-fashioned quotations she dished out with our oatmeal. The first was Shakespeare: "To thine own self be true, and it must follow as the night the day, Thou canst not then be false to any man." The second was Sir Walter Scott: "Oh, what a tangled web we weave, when first we practice to deceive!"

Once you start it, there's no place that deception can stop — and of course it has to start with self-deception, even if it's only the self-deception of believing we can get away with it. True, sometimes we are not "discovered." But all of modern psychology and psychiatry is based on the belief that our self-deceptions drive things into our subconscious where they make all kinds of trouble. . . .

Live with Enthusiasm: It has been my experience that there is nothing worth doing that can be done without it. Ability you must have, but ability sparked with enthusiasm. Enthusiasm is an inexhaustible force, so mighty that you must ever tame and temper it with wisdom. Use it and you will find yourself constantly moving forward to new forms of expression.

If you have enthusiasm for life you cannot ever know an inactive time of life. Sir Christopher Wren, the famed architect who built fifty-two churches in London, retired from public life at eighty-six. After that he spent five years in literary, astronomical and religious pursuits. Cato, at eighty, studied Greek; and Plutarch, almost as old, Latin. Titian painted a masterpiece at ninety-eight. Verdi wrote his great opera, *Othello*, at seventy-four, and *Falstaff* at eighty. What is that but continued enthusiasm for life?

Everyone faces hardships along their chosen path. What carries them through? Makes them work and pray with no thought of quitting? Enthusiasm! After working long and hard to accumulate his first $50, Frank Woolworth saw three of his first five chain stores fail. The *Saturday Evening Post* lost $800,000 for Cyrus H. K. Curtis before a single dollar of profit came in. Twenty-seven million dollars and eleven years of work were behind the first pound of Nylon sold by DuPont.

There is no such thing as being "a little bit enthusiastic." You either are or aren't. If you aren't you face failure and boredom. You can't take it by the spoonful. . . .

Don't Let Your Possessions Possess You: I have in my lifetime had everything—and nothing. In my Bible it doesn't say that money is the root of all evil, but the "*love of*" money. I believe that to be true and I believe the exact same to be true about possessions.

They are very nice to have, to enjoy, to share. But if you find even one that you can't live without—hasten to give it away. Your very freedom depends on it.

We have all heard of the lack of sense of the monkey who will put his paw into the narrow mouth of a bottle, grasp a desired nut or bit of food, and refuse to let it go even though the fist he has made makes his hand too large to draw it from the bottle again. "Silly thing," we say, "he hasn't really got the food— and he's attached to the bottle. All he has to do is open his hand and let go."

We laugh. But is it so funny? The monkey has lost his freedom. Do we guard ourselves from falling into the same trap?

Don't Worry about Your Problems: The successful life is a balanced life and includes thought, action, rest, recreation. The artist in living will neither work himself to death nor play until he reaches satiety. Now the chronic worrier is all out of balance. He is like a dog with a bone. Problems, and we all have them, are puzzles offered us for solution and we solve them by keeping in balance, alert mentally and well physically, or we handicap ourselves. To worry your difficulties after the sun is set and you have done all you can for the day is useless—and an act of distrust. . . .

Don't Cling to the Past: Not through regret. Not through longing. To do so is to tie yourself to a memory, for yesterday is gone. It is wisdom to profit by yesterday's mistakes. It is fatal to hang onto yesterday's victories. You limit yourself. The future should be expanding. Yesterday's experiences are the foundation on which you build today.

A man walking with his eyes turned backward is very apt to fall into a ditch. It has been said that I would never part with certain hotels. This is not true. If I have had to let go of a success (and I have had to many times) to build an expanding future, then I've released yesterday. We can only act *now* and then look forward to more activity, greater fulfillment.

To be haunted by past failures or satisfied with past successes is to arrest forward motion. . . .

Look Up to People When You Can—Down to No One: Who and what is your neighbor? Do you know him?

Let's take a man standing at 50th Street and Park Avenue in New York City; he is waiting for the light to turn. Who is he? To the statistician standing at the window high above, he is one unit in a crowd. To the biologist he is a specimen; to the physicist a formula of mass and energy; to the chemist a compound of substances. He is of interest to the historian as one of the billions of beings who have inhabited this planet of ours; to the politician as a vote; to the merchandiser as a customer;

to the mailman as an address. The behaviorist sees him from his office across the street and tags him as an animal modified by conditioned reflexes; and the psychiatrist in the next suite as a particular mental type deviating in one way or another from the alleged normal.

> ### *Extreme Measures*
> To finance his growing hotel empire, Hilton borrowed against his own life insurance policy, even though he had a wife and three children to worry about should the worst happen.

Each science pinpoints the poor fellow from some particular angle and makes him look foolish, like the candid camera shot that catches you in the middle of a yawn. Let any one of these specialists pigeonhole you and get you to look at yourself through his single eye and what you will see will not be a man, but a fragment of a man. . . .

As we strive to know more about people, to understand rather than to be understood, we are in a better position to fulfill the commandment to "love our neighbor as ourselves."

Assume Your Full Share of Responsibility for the World in Which You Live: Develop your own policy, domestic and foreign. Give it thought. And then effort. Stand on it! Stand for it! Live it!

The whole purpose of democracy is for the participation of the individual. The will of the people. You cannot have "government of the people, by the people, for the people" without the active participation of those people.

Nor can your life be a personal success unless, as a citizen, tourist, voter, you share in shaping your own world. . . .

The successful American will not be indifferent. He will let his enthusiasms sweep into his patriotism and be an *individual* cog in the wheels that lead to a better world. President Eisenhower has truly said: "We are not helpless prisoners of history. We are free men." But only so long as the individual desires it! And works for it!

Henry J. Kaiser

Industrialist Henry Kaiser's firm was a major partner in building both the great Boulder and Grand Coulee dams, and he became a World War II hero due to his company's shipbuilding achievements. To help support the family, he dropped out of school at age 11 and was an errand boy for a local photographer. Before reaching age 20, Kaiser had saved enough money to buy the photographer out. In 1906, he became a salesman for a construction company, and in 1913, he founded his own street paving company. Kaiser, who had great faith in himself, soon moved into heavy construction and the manufacturing of steel, aluminum, and cement, among other ventures. Boulder Dam was completed in 1935 and Coulee in 1941. When World War II started, his company had never built a ship, but went on to construct almost 1,500.

Imagine Your Future

1. *Know yourself and decide what you want most of all to make out of your life. Then write down your goals and a plan to reach them.*

   What would you rather accomplish than anything else in the world?

Do you want to be a millionaire?—And if so, I hope you will include becoming a *millionaire in the real things of life,* as well as in money. Do you want to become a great engineer, teacher, businessman, industrialist, statesman, farmer, or home-maker, or what?

Before you can decide clearly and rightly upon your inmost desires in life, you need to analyze what you have to offer. . . .

2. *Use the great powers that you can tap through faith in God and the hidden energies of your soul and sub-conscious mind.*

Over and over, in an infinite number and variety of proofs in the lives of folks, I have seen how man can draw upon the High Power and the soul within him.

Call it the sub-conscious mind or the soul, there is in every human being a reservoir of inspiration and intuitions—the source from which spring the emotions and the driving force for good.

3. *Love people and serve them.*

This is practical. I can think of hundreds of successful persons whose careers prove that it works. A pervading, fundamental love of people—all people—is an unfailing mark of the finest characters. An ingrained attitude of, "What will I get out of it?" leads up a blind alley to failure.

4. *Develop your positive traits of character and personality.*

You don't have to blow the top off an I.Q. test or be the son or daughter of genius to succeed. You don't have to be at the head of your class, in order to pass by the

---

Smart Habits

To keep a positive mental attitude, Kaiser adopted "Oh, What a Beautiful Morning" as his number one theme song.

ones who were first in grades but lacking in fundamental aspects of character and personality.

5. *Work! Put your life's plan into determined action and go after what you want with all that's in you.*

My mother used to say to me from the days of my earliest memories, "Henry, nothing ever is accomplished without work. If I left you nothing else but a will to work, I would leave you the most priceless gift."

B. C. Forbes
1880–1954

*T*he founder of Forbes *magazine and a publishing empire was 1 of 10 children born to a tailor in Scotland. At the age of 14, B. C. Forbes agreed to a seven-year apprenticeship as a compositor for a local newspaper, thinking he'd learn to write, but to his chagrin, he discovered it meant grueling typesetting work. So he took a shorthand writing course (a prerequisite for journalists) and convinced the newspaper to make him a reporter. In 1902, he left Scotland for South Africa in search of adventure during the Boer War, which pitted Great Britain against white South Africans. In 1904, Forbes immigrated to the United States, where he found work in New York City, writing for several publications. Forbes founded his namesake in 1917, and after years of rubbing elbows with top executives and managing his own business, he developed quite a checklist for success.*

Keys to Success

Your success depends upon you.
Your happiness depends upon you.
You have to steer your own course.
You have to shape your own fortune.
You have to educate yourself.

You have to do your own thinking.

You have to live with your own conscience.

Your mind is yours and can be used only by you.

You come into the world alone.

You go to the grave alone.

You are alone with your inner thoughts during the journey between.

You must make your own decisions.

You must abide by the consequences of your acts.

"I cannot make you well unless you make yourself well," an eminent doctor often tells his patients.

You alone can regulate your habits and make or unmake your health.

You alone can assimilate things mental and things material.

Said a Brooklyn preacher, offering his parishioners communion one Sunday: "I cannot give you the blessings and the benefits of this holy feast. You must appropriate them for yourselves. The banquet is spread; help yourself freely.

"You may be invited to a feast where the table is laden with the choicest foods, but unless you partake of the foods, unless you appropriate and assimilate them, they can do you no good. So it is with this holy feast. You must appropriate its blessings. I cannot infuse them into you."

You have to do your own assimilation all through life.

You may be taught by a teacher, but you have to imbibe the knowledge. He cannot transfuse it into your brain.

You alone can control your mind cells and your brain cells.

You may have spread before you the wisdom of the ages, but unless you assimilate it you derive no benefit from it; no one can force it into your cranium.

You alone can move your own legs.

You alone can use your own arms.

You alone can utilize your own hands.

You alone can control your own muscles.

You must stand on your feet, physically and metaphorically.

You must take your own steps.

Your parents cannot enter into your skin, take control of your mental and physical machinery, and make something of you.

You cannot fight your son's battles; that he must do for himself.

You have to be captain of your own destiny.

You have to see through your own eyes.

You have to use your own ears.

You have to master your own faculties.

You have to solve your own problems.

You have to form your own ideals.

You have to create your own ideas.

Smart Habits

Don't be afraid to kick your feet up on your desk, close your eyes, and do some serious thinking, Forbes advised. At the very least, Forbes said that one or two nights a week should be dedicated to intense thought about both business and life. In the hustle and bustle of the world, not enough people set aside time for undisturbed, reflective thinking.

You must choose your own speech.

You must govern your own tongue.

Your real life is your thoughts.

Your thoughts are of your own making.

Your character is your own handiwork.

You alone can select the materials that go into it.

You alone can reject what is not fit to go into it.

You are the creator of your own personality.

You can be disgraced by no man's hand but your own.

You can be elevated and sustained by no man save yourself.

You have to write your own record.

You have to build your own monument—or dig your own pit.

Which are you doing?

B enjamin Franklin is the archetypal American entrepreneur and businessman, and is renowned for his puritan maxims that appeared in his Poor Richard's Almanac. It did not come easy. Franklin was a poor student who failed in math, and at the age of 12, he was forced into an apprenticeship under his older brother, a printer, that was supposed to last until he was 21. By age 17, Franklin had had enough, and escaped Boston for Philadelphia, where he worked for another printer before he founded the Pennsylvania Gazette in 1728 and built a renowned print shop. He printed books, started Gazettes in Rhode Island and South Carolina, became the "public" printer for several states, and published the priceless Poor Richard's Almanac from 1732 to 1757 — not to mention that he was a respected diplomat and helped draft the Declaration of Independence.

Thirteen Virtues

1. TEMPERANCE
   Eat not to dullness; drink not to elevation.

2. SILENCE
   Speak not but what may benefit others or yourself; avoid trifling conversation.

3. ORDER
Let all your things have their places; let each part of your business have its time.

4. RESOLUTION
Resolve to perform what you ought; perform without fail what you resolve.

5. FRUGALITY
Make no expense but to do good to others or yourself; *i.e.*, waste nothing.

6. INDUSTRY
Lose no time; be always employ'd in something useful; cut off all unnecessary actions.

7. SINCERITY
Use no hurtful deceit; think innocently and justly; and, if you speak, speak accordingly.

8. JUSTICE
Wrong none by doing injuries, or omitting the benefits that are your duty.

9. MODERATION
Avoid extreams; forbear resenting injuries so much as you think they deserve.

10. CLEANLINESS
Tolerate no uncleanliness in body, cloaths, or habitation.

Smart Habits

Franklin made a grid with the days of the week across the top and 13 virtues down the side, and at the end of each day he would mark what virtues he had violated. Each week he would focus on a particular virtue, hoping that after a 13-week period he would have much greater strength of character.

TEMPERANCE. EAT NOT TO DULLNESS; DRINK NOT TO ELEVATION.							
	S.	M.	T.	W.	T.	F.	S.
T.							
S.	*	*		*		*	
O.	**	*	*		*	*	*
R.			*			*	
F.		*			*		
I.			*				
S.							
J.							
M.							
C.							
T.							
C.							
H.							

11. TRANQUILLITY

Be not disturbed at trifles, or at accidents common or unavoidable.

12. CHASTITY

Rarely use venery but for health or offspring, never to dulness, weakness, or the injury of your own or another's peace or reputation.

13. HUMILITY

Imitate Jesus and Socrates.

The precept of *Order* requiring that *every part of my business should have its allotted time,* one page in my little book contain'd the following scheme of employment for the twenty-four hours of a natural day.

THE MORNING. *Question.* What good shall I do this day?	5 6 ⎱ ⎰ 7	Rise, wash, and address *Powerful Goodness!* Contrive day's business, and take the resolution of the day; prosecute the present study, and breakfast.
	8 9 10 11	Work.
NOON.	12 1	Read, or overlook my accounts, and dine.
	2 3 4 5	Work.
EVENING. *Question.* What good have I done to-day?	6 7 8 9	Put things in their places. Supper. Music or diversion, or conversation. Examination of the day.
	10 11 12	
NIGHT.	1 2 3 4	Sleep.

Acknowledgments

I was having lunch with Ed Knappman, my agent, and naming all the business legends who had their own unique list of habits and/or tips for success. Surely, I said, the lists could be combined to create the ultimate capitalist manifesto. Ed responded: "The better book would be a collection of those lists, plain and simple." He was right, and I tip my hat to Ed. Thanks also to my good friend, Ruth Mills, who took on the project, and to Airié Dekidjiev, who is now my caretaker. It's also very important to acknowledge the many authors and editors who had the foresight to distill respective business philosophies to the pithy templates found in this book. As always, thanks to Sasha Kintzler, to many others at John Wiley & Sons whom I have yet to meet, and to North Market Street Graphics. Diana, Pierson, Alex, and Julia—you're the best.

Credits and Sources

"Man in the Mirror Test" from *Live to Win* by Victor Kiam. Copyright © 1990 by Victor Kiam. Reprinted by permission of HarperCollins Publishers, Inc.

"The Final Checklist" from *One Up on Wall Street* by Peter Lynch. Copyright © 1989 by Peter Lynch. Reprinted by permission of Simon & Schuster.

"The Ten Most Toxic Lies in Business" from *Success Secrets* by Mark McCormack. Used by permission of Christine Pauletta and IMG.

"Creating a Productive Climate" by Rene McPherson, from *Leaders*, March 1980. Copyright © 1980.

"Basic Components for Success" from *Harvest of Joy, My Passion, My Life* by Robert Mondavi. Copyright © 1998 by Robert Mondavi. Reprinted by permission of Harcourt, Inc.

"An S.O.B.'s Ten Secrets to Success" from *Confessions of an S.O.B.* by Al Neuharth. Copyright © 1989 by Al Neuharth. Used by permission of Doubleday, a division of Random House, Inc.

"Qualities I Admire" from *Confessions of an Advertising Man* by David Ogilvy. Copyright © 1963 David Ogilvy Trustee. Reprinted with the permission of Scribner, a division of Simon & Schuster.

"Principles of Idea-Conveying" by John H. Patterson, from *System: The Magazine of Business*, June 1918.

"Six Principles" from *Fifty Years with the Golden Rule* by J. C. Penney. Published by Harper & Brothers, 1950.

"Eight Attributes of Innovative Companies" from *In Search of Excellence* by Thomas J. Peters and Robert H. Waterman, Jr. Copyright © 1982 by Thomas J. Peters and Robert H. Waterman, Jr. Reprinted by permission of HarperCollins Publishers, Inc.

"The Art of Leadership" by T. Boone Pickens, from *Fortune*, February 16, 1987. Copyright © Time Inc. Reprinted by permission.

"The American Businessman" from *Random Reminiscences of Men and Events* by John D. Rockefeller. Published by Doubleday, Page & Company, 1909.

"Starbucks Mission Statement" and "Capturing the Customer's Imagination" from *Pour Your Heart Into It* by Howard Schultz and Dori Jones Yang. Copyright © 1997 Howard Schultz and Dori Jones Yang. Published by Hyperion, 1997.

"The Bottom Line of Mutual Funds" from *Charles Schwab's Guide to Financial Freedom* by Charles R. Schwab. Copyright © 1998 by The Charles Schwab Corporation. Reprinted by permission of Crown Publishers, a division of Random House, Inc.

"Some Outlandish Rules for Making Money" from *Damned Old Crank* by E. W. Scripps. Copyright 1951 by Harper & Brothers. Reprinted by Permission of HarperCollins Publishers, Inc.

"The GE Values Guide" from *Jack Welch and the GE Way* by Robert Slater. Copyright © 1998 by Robert Slater. Used by permission of The McGraw-Hill Companies.

"The Time-tested Maxims of the Templeton Touch" by Sir John Templeton, from *The Templeton Touch* by William Proctor. Copyright © 1983. Used by permission of John Templeton.

"Dave's Rules for Successful Harassment" from *Dave's Way* by David Thomas. Copyright © 1991 by R. David Thomas.

"No-No's" from *Up the Organization* by Robert Townsend. Copyright © 1970 by Robert Townsend. Reprinted by permission of Alfred A. Knopf, a division of Random House, Inc.

"The Making of a Businessman" by Theodore Vail, from *Youth's Companion*, September 1913.

"Are You an Entrepreneur?" from *An Eye for Winners* by Lillian Vernon. Copyright © 1996 by Lillian Vernon. Reprinted by permission of HarperCollins Publishers, Inc.

Author Index

Subject Index